Hippie Crafts

Library of Congress Cataloging-in-Publication Data

O'Sullivan, Joanne.
  Hippie crafts : creating a hip new look using groovy '60s crafts / by
Joanne O'Sullivan.-- 1st ed.
    p. cm.
  Includes index.
  ISBN 1-57990-603-6 (pbk.)
 1. Handicraft. 2. Hippies. 3. Nineteen sixties. I. Title.
TT157.O8323 2004
745.5--dc22

                                                           2004003495

10 9 8 7 6 5 4 3 2 1

First Edition

Published by Lark Books, A Division of
Sterling Publishing Co., Inc.
387 Park Avenue South, New York, N.Y. 10016

© 2004, Lark Books
Distributed in Canada by Sterling Publishing,
c/o Canadian Manda Group, One Atlantic Ave., Suite 105
Toronto, Ontario, Canada M6K 3E7

Distributed in the U.K. by Guild of Master Craftsman Publications Ltd.,
Castle Place, 166 High Street, Lewes, East Sussex, England
BN7 1XU
Tel: (+ 44) 1273 477374, Fax: (+ 44) 1273 478606, Email: pubs@thegmc-
group.com, Web: www.gmcpublications.com

Distributed in Australia by Capricorn Link (Australia) Pty Ltd.,
P.O. Box 704, Windsor, NSW 2756 Australia

If you have questions or comments about this book, please contact:
Lark Books
67 Broadway
Asheville, NC 28801
(828) 253-0467

Manufactured in China

ISBN 1-57990-603-6

Senior Editor: PAIGE GILCHRIST

Art Director: DANA MARGARET IRWIN

Photographer: SANDRA STAMBAUGH

Cover Designer: BARBARA ZARETSKY

Associate Editor: REBECCA LIM

Assistant Art Director: LANCE WILLE

Illustrator: ORRIN LUNDGREN

Editorial Assistance: DELORES GOSNELL,
ROSEMARY KAST, JEFF HAMILTON,
KALIN SIEGWALD

Hippie Crafts

Creating a Hip New Look Using Groovy '60s Crafts

Joanne O'Sullivan

LARK BOOKS

A Division of Sterling Publishing Co., Inc.
New York

Contents

joyful jazz
theater
(a non-spectator event)

the howard hanger trio

WWW.MOTHEREARTHNEWS.COM

INTRODUCTION

AP/WIDE WORLD PHOTO

ROBERT SMELTZER PHOTO

WITHIN YOU WITHOUT YOU

There are two immutable truths about style. The first is that it's fickle. Materials and color palettes come and go in the blink of an eye. What's in today will be hopelessly *out* tomorrow. The second is that what goes around comes around. If you hold on to anything long enough, it *will* come back in, this time with that much more panache for being authentic. Such is the case with hippie styles. The unique, funky, and wildly creative clothing and decor of the '60s were the butt of many jokes once the glittery disco era got underway in the mid-'70s. Handmade clothes, worn-out denims, and beaded curtains? No self-respecting disco diva would be caught dead around them. In the *Dynasty* decade of the '80s, hippie style fared no better. At last, in the new millennium, hippie is a style whose time has come again (with new colors and other updated elements).

POWER TO

All you need is love

If you lived through the '60s, you'll be happy to see your old favorites again. If you didn't, here's your chance to find out what it was all about.

Being a hippie meant (among other things) rejecting the establishment, being self-reliant, and most of all, being creative. That spirit of freedom and individuality led a lot of people to learn new skills, take up crafts, and make everything possible instead of buying it. From jewelry and clothes to furniture and even houses, do-it-yourself was the hippie way. Time passed, though, and

the '80s happened. All things hippie became passé. But some enthusiasts kept the hippie spirit alive, and now a new generation is rediscovering hippie styles and the satisfaction that comes from making them by hand.

Remember that groovy crocheted shawl you wore every day in the winter of '68? It's on page 46, except instead of the rainbow-colored yarn you made it with, we've used a *tasteful* variegated yarn in sage green.

PHOTOS,
TOP TO BOTTOM:
© TED STRESHINKSY/CORBIS,
DANA IRWIN,
© AP/WIDE WORLD PHOTO

KEEP THE FAITH, BABY

Okay, so maybe you weren't even born in '68. Ever see a picture of your favorite '60s rock star in a leather fringed vest? You can easily make one yourself, using the instructions on page 86. This book covers classic hippie designs in eight crafts: sewing, tie-dye/batik, crochet, macramé, leather crafts, jewelry, weaving and yarn crafts, and candlemaking. While you'll recognize the source of the inspiration, we've reinter-

preted the old standards with new colors, materials, and embellishments that say *today*.

Some of the projects in the book are for those with special skills (the crochet and macramé projects are not for beginners), while others require only the right materials and a willingness to try. If you knew how to crochet or macramé once upon a time but have forgotten, the reference section will refresh your memory with clear illustrations for basic crochet stitches and macramé knots.

Just for fun and to provide you with a little nostalgia, you'll find great period photos throughout the book, along with some historical background to set the scene. While your first reaction may be to have a good laugh and exclaim "What were they thinking?" you may be surprised by how fresh and *interesting* hippie style still looks today.

Before you get started making projects, read Hippies 101, a flashback on hippie history that sets the mood.

Keep on

Hippies 101

What Is a Hippie?

The mid-'60s found parents, pundits, and politicians scratching their heads, asking this same question. As far as anyone could tell, an entire generation, which had grown up with comfort, stability, and education (all the things the previous generation strived for), had collectively thumbed their noses at prevailing cultural values. The media portrayed them as dirty, lazy, pot-smoking freeloaders with radical ideas. It was clear what the hippies didn't want: a conformist lifestyle, a materialistic society, a life spent living to work instead of working to live. But what did they want? Most said it was freedom: freedom to express themselves through the clothes they wore, the music they listened to, and the way they lived. They wanted peace, inside and out in the war-torn world. They wanted community and real connections between people, a world where people shared what they had. They wanted respect: for themselves, for the earth, and for differences between people. And finally, they wanted love as the foundation for interactions between people of all types. So, who were the hippies—idealists, dreamers, or deluded dropouts? History has proven that there was a little bit of truth to all the characterizations of the '60s youth, both positive and negative. But there's no doubt that they had an effect and in some measure achieved their goal of making the world a better place.

"truckin'"

light is love

AMERICA
ADULT TOUR
MISTAKE
WITHDRAW THE TROOPS

PEACE
LOVE
HAPP-
INESS

Talkin' 'Bout My Generation
Hippie Lingo

Like all subcultures, the hippie counterculture developed its own words, phrases, and ways of speaking that only the in-group members knew.

Some hippie lingo has been absorbed into mainstream language, used daily by young and old alike. Other words and expressions, which once had the ring of rebellion to them, have been retired from use, existing now as quaint reminders of a bygone era.

Acid. LSD, a narcotic drug popular among hippies.

Be into. To enjoy or take part in. Example: "She's really into yoga."

Blow your mind. To have an enlightening or illuminating experience.

Bread. Money.

Bummer. Bad experience.

Bust. An arrest (usually related to drug arrests).

Cat. A person, usually a guy (derived from beatnik language of the '50s)

Chick. A girl or woman.

Cool. Good.

Crash. To sleep, rest, or do nothing.

Crash pad. A place where one sleeps, rests, or does nothing.

Dig. Like, enjoy, be interested in, or understand.

Dough. Money.

Downer. A negative experience.

Drag. A negative experience. Example: "It's kind of a drag when your baby don't love you."

Far out. Exciting, different, and interesting. Also used as an exclamation.

Flower power. The power of love and peace.

Freak. As a noun, used to describe one who is excessively "into" something. Example: "He's a speed freak." As a verb, used to describe having paranoid delusions.

Fuzz. The police.

Get it on. Usually used to describe having sex, but sometimes used to describe relating to people.

Gig. Performance, show, or steady activity, such as a job. Example: "I've got a carpentry gig."

Grass. Marijuana, pot, weed.

Groove on. To enjoy. Example: "She was really grooving on the music."

Groovy. Good, cool, hip.

Hang out. To be somewhere, doing nothing in particular.

Hang-up. Inhibition, usually due to morals, beliefs, or culture.

Happening. As an adjective, exciting, new, good. Example: "There's a happening new band in town." As a noun, an event, sometimes spontaneous, usually involving art, music, or performance.

Head shop. A store that sells drug paraphanalia and posters.

Heat. The police.

Heavy. Deep, interesting, and thought provoking.

Hip. In the know.

Let it all hang out. Relax.

Like. Word used to fill up space when the speaker is unable to think of a suitable adjective to describe something.

Love beads. Colorful beads worn around the neck to symbolize love.

Man. As a noun, used to describe the establishment. Example: "The man is always trying to put us down." As an interjection, used for emphasis. Example: "Man, I could really use some dough."

Narc. Originally used to describe the drug police; eventually used to describe a person who informs the police about illegal activities or drug use, or anyone who gives away a secret.

Out of sight. Really great. Usually used as an exclamation, but sometimes as an adjective.

Pad. A place to live.

Pot. See grass.

Psychedelic. An adjective used to describe something reminiscent of the hallucinations experienced while on LSD, that is, intense colors or sounds, distorted perceptions, or surreal visions.

Put down. Insult.

Rap. To have a conversation or just talk extemporaneously.

Right on. Used as an exclamation of agreement. Example: "You're moving to 'Frisco? Right on!"

Rip off. As a noun, a scam. As a verb, to steal from someone.

Shack up. For a couple, to live together without getting married.

Sock it to me. Tell me or let me have it.

Spaced out. Not alert.

Split. To leave.

Square. Old-fashioned or conformist.

Trip. Usually used to describe an experience after taking acid, but also used to describe other experiences. Example: "That guy is really on an ego trip."

Turn on. To become aware of or experience. Also used to describe being high on drugs.

Uptight. Not open to new ideas.

Vibe. Atmosphere or spirit.

Weed. See grass.

PHOTOS: TOP TO BOTTOM:
© BETTMAN/CORBIS
© BETTMAN/CORBIS
COURTESY OF JERRY KAMSTRA

Cellophane flowers of yellow and green...

Sewing

n the '50s, "she makes her own clothes" was a veiled insult: It meant the woman in question was a bit frumpy and old-fashioned and didn't have enough money to buy the latest fashions. But in the '60s, all that changed. Being able to make your own clothes was cool—a way to be self-reliant, individual, and unique; and best of all, it was a way to reject consumer products being pedaled

by the establishment. Any hippie girl could show you how to turn old jeans into a skirt, make straight legs into bell-bottoms, or patch over worn denim. It was easy to make halter tops from bandanas or scarves, or make simple ponchos or capes. Those who were even more skilled made their own peasant dresses, patch-work skirts, and quilts. If you missed the '60s and never learned, or have since forgotten how to make these old favorites, this chapter will give you the instructions you need to recreate them or try them for the very first time.

Big photo: Dresses by Becky Biller.
Left to right: Cape by Jean Ray Laury, shirts by Joyce Aiken,
dress by Jean Ray Laury.
PHOTOS COURTESY OF JEAN RAY LAURY AND JOYCE AIKEN

Mountain Girl Poncho

Was there a single hippie girl who didn't have a fringed poncho? You don't have to weave your own fabric for this one. It's made with an inexpensive throw blanket and a few simple stitches on a sewing machine.

You Will Need

4 1/2 x 6-foot (1.3 x 1.8 m) woven throw with fringe

Measuring tape

Straight pins

Sewing machine with zigzag stitch

Matching thread

Scissors

1 Fold the throw in half so the fringe on the 4 1/2-foot (1.3 m) sides meet.

2 Fold the throw in half again so the other sides meet. The inside corner of the fold is the center of the neck.

3 Measure 7 inches (17.8 cm) in each direction from the center point. Mark with pins. This place is where you'll make the neck hole, which should be parallel to the fringe.

4 Open the throw and straight-stitch around the pins in an oval shape. Your stitches should be about 1/2 inch (1.3 cm) apart. Now do a zigzag stitch next to the straight stitch. Use a wide zigzag with the stitches close together. This will keep the neck from unraveling when you cut it open.

5 Cut through the center of the 1/2 x 14-inch (1.3 x 35.6 cm) oval. This opens the neck hole.

6 Fold over the edges of the neck hole twice, and straight-stitch in place.

7 Zigzag all around the edge of the neck hole. Repeat until the edges are covered.

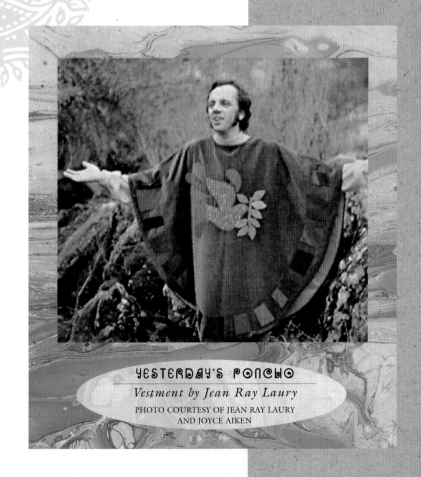

YESTERDAY'S PONCHO
Vestment by Jean Ray Laury
PHOTO COURTESY OF JEAN RAY LAURY AND JOYCE AIKEN

Skirt instructions on page 18

Roadhouse Blues Bell-Bottoms

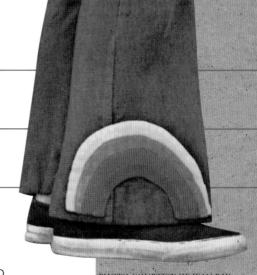

PHOTO COURTESY OF JEAN RAY LAURY AND JOYCE AIKEN

a uniquely hippie phenomenon, bell-bottoms were born when thrifty kids went scrounging for cheap clothes in army-navy surplus stores and started wearing wide-legged wool sailor pants. The fashion caught on and was translated into bell-bottom jeans. No hippie was without a pair. If you have trouble finding them today, make your own from conventional straight legs.

1 Using the seam ripper, rip the outside seam of the jeans from the hem to the knee.

2 Use the tape measure to find the measurements for the patterned fabric insert. The width measurement of the patterned fabric insert equals the circumference of the leg. The length of the fabric should be 1 inch (2.5 cm) longer than the length of the ripped seam. Fold the fabric in half and cut a triangle from the top edge of the fold to the bottom edge of the selvage.

3 Turn the jeans inside out. Pin the fabric to the opening, lining up the point of the fabric with the end of the ripped seam near the knee, leaving a ¼-inch (6 mm) seam allowance.

4 With the right sides together, sew the fabric to the jeans along the ripped seam, reenforcing the corner at the ripped knee.

5 Repeat with the other leg.

6 Cut two small pieces of fabric into a rectangle 1 inch (2.5 cm) wider and 2 inches (5.2 cm) longer than the opening of the front jeans pocket.

7 Fold a ¼-inch (6 mm) seam under the fabric piece under and hand-stitch it to the bottom edge of the waistband in the pocket opening.

8 Spread fabric glue on the back of the fabric piece and adhere it to the exposed inside panel of the pocket. Fold the outside edge of the piece of fabric in ¼ inch (6 mm) and hand-stitch the fabric to the outside seam of the jeans. Tuck the excess fabric into the pocket.

9 Repeat with the other front pocket.

You Will Need

Seam ripper

Old jeans

Tape measure

1½ yards (1.3 m) of patterned fabric

Scissors

Straight pins

Fabric glue

Sewing machine (optional)

Sewing needle and thread

Designer: *Joan Morris*

Forever in Blue Jeans Skirt

in the spirit of recycling, hippie girls made good use out of old blue jeans by turning them into skirts. The look is still fresh today, and it's an easy project.

1 Use the seam ripper to take out the entire inseam of the jeans. Most jeans have a rolled seam and two rows of stitching—you'll need to take out both.

2 Remove the seam from the zipper down. Remove the rear seam from the inseam up about 6 inches (15.2 cm).

3 Lay the jeans flat on a table, face up. Position the open seam under the zipper, with the left leg over the right. This will create a triangle between the legs. Measure the size of the triangle and write down the measurement. Pin everything in place and machine-stitch two rows of stitching to hold the position.

4 Turn the jeans over (back side up). Position the open seam, placing the right leg over the left. Pin in place, turning under the edges. Machine-stitch two rows to match the front.

5 Turn the pants over again so that the front is facing up. Cut a piece of fabric ½ inch (1.3 cm) wider and 1 inch (2.5 cm) longer than the measurement you wrote down in step 3. Fold the hem under twice and machine-stitch in place.

6 Pin the triangle in place and machine-stitch two rows to hold it in place.

Repeat steps 5 and 6 on the back of the jeans. The only difference is you must fold under the edge of the jean seam.

You Will Need

Seam ripper

Pair of jeans

Measuring tape

Paper and pencil

Straight pins

Sewing machine

Matching thread

Scissors

1 yard (91.4 cm) patterned fabric

YESTERDAY'S JEANS SKIRT

Skirt by Pat Haines

PHOTO COURTESY OF ALEXANDRA
JACOPETTI HART
AND THE ESTATE OF JERRY WAINWRIGHT

Designer: *Joan Morris*

Instant Karma Pillow Covers

if you're a little nervous about hanging your Indian print tapestry over a ceiling fixture like they did in the old days, there are plenty of other things you can do with it. The fabric is perfect for pillow covers that add just a touch of hippie chic to your decor.

Square Design Pillow

1. To make the pillow with a square in the center, fold the fabric to make four triangles, each with the striped border at the bottom and the paisley at the top. With the measuring tape, make sure the size of the triangles equals the size of the pillow plus 1 inch (2.5 cm) all the way around for the seam allowance.

2. Cut out the four triangles and lay them flat in position on top of the pillow form. Take two of the triangles and place them right sides together, matching the stripe in the design. Pin them together and machine-stitch the seam, allowing a 1/2 inch (1.3 cm) for seam allowance. Press the seam open.

3. Repeat step 2 for the opposite two triangles.

4. Pin together the two sewn halves, matching the pattern in the center. Sew the seam. Press the seam open. You now have the front of the pillow.

5. Cut out two pieces of the paisley fabric the same size as the front piece.

6. On one end of each piece, fold over a 1-inch (2.5 cm) section twice to make a hem, and stitch.

7. Lay the top piece face up. Now lay one of the hemmed pieces face down with the hem about 4 inches (10.2 cm) from one side. Place the other hemmed piece face down 4 inches (10.2 cm) from the other side in the opposite direction. Pin in place. Stitch all the way around the pinned pieces. Cut off any excess fabric.

8. Turn the piece right side out and push out the corners. You have made an opening in which to place the pillow form without a zipper.

9. Stuff the pillow form into the pillow cover. With the matching thread, hand-stitch the last side closed.

Striped Pillow Cover

1. To make the striped pillow, cut out two strips of the striped part of the fabric and three strips of the paisley. Make one of the paisley strips larger for the center. Don't forget to cut enough for all the seam allowances.

2. Sew all the strips together and press the seams open.

3. Repeat steps 5 through 9, left, to complete the pillow cover.

Indian Print Fabric Scarf

If you're looking for a use for extra scraps from your Indian tapestry fabric, you can very easily make a headscarf. Measure the distance between your ears, starting at one ear, across the top of your head to the other ear. Draw a light pencil line onto the fabric the same length as this measurement for the long end of the triangle, and then use a ruler to draw the other sides to make the point. Cut out the triangle and fold and press a 1/4-inch (1.3 cm) seam under, then sew. Cut two strips of fabric for the ties, and sew them onto the points on the long end of the triangle.

You Will Need

Indian paisley tapestry with striped borders

Measuring tape

Scissors

12-inch (31 cm) square pillow forms

Straight pins

Sewing machine

Iron and ironing board

Matching thread and needle

Hippie Chic
Head to Toe Hippie Fashion

For some, being a hippie was a state of mind, an attitude, and a way of life. For others, it was a fashion statement.

Up until the early '60s, hairstyles and clothing in North America (and to a lesser extent in Europe) were more or less homogenous. Fashion houses in New York and Paris dictated the lengths of hemlines for women and the style of suits for men. Men wore their hair in crew cuts and women wore bouffants or beehives held in place with liberal doses of hairspray.

Then the Beatles arrived on the scene with their "mop tops," scandalizing the older generation and starting a fashion revolution.

What started out as a hairstyle became a symbol of nonconformity for the entire generation. A new, cool hairstyle was the first step towards fashion liberation. Women let their hair grow long and stopped styling it (some even stopped washing it). The hair accessories of choice were garlands of flowers or headbands worn around the forehead. Men let their hair grow longer and longer, and they grew sideburns, beards, and mustaches. Before the term hippie became widespread, the older generation referred to the rebellious youth simply as "longhairs." African American men and women stopped straightening their hair and let it grow out naturally—a style that became known as the Afro.

For fashion inspiration, Paris and New York were out; San Francisco and London were in. But most hippies would describe themselves as antifashion. They wore whatever seemed groovy. Women wore their hemlines up or down, from miniskirts and hot pants to maxiskirts and granny dresses. Instead of emulating the wealthy and well groomed, they sought out peasant clothes and ethnic looks. Peasant blouses, gypsy skirts, ponchos, serapes, and saris were trendy for women, while men wore Nehru jackets. Caftans and dashikis were worn by both sexes, accessorized with long strings of "love beads," Native American-inspired beaded necklaces, or peace-symbol pendants.

Raleigh and his new Greek shirt, Samos, Greece, 1972
PHOTO BY DANA IRWIN

Instead of shopping in big department stores, kids flocked to surplus and thrift stores for secondhand clothes they could salvage and rework for a unique look. They turned jeans into bell-bottoms, patched them up with peace symbols or hearts, or created entirely new clothing out of patches of different clothes; they added tassels and fringe to castaway clothes to dress them up.

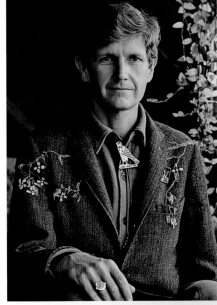

PHOTO COURTESY OF ALEXANDRA JACOPETTI HART AND THE ESTATE OF JERRY WAINWRIGHT

"The natural look" replaced the dramatic makeup, false eyelashes, and stylized hairdos worn by the Mods. Women wore no makeup, got rid of their bras, and stopped shaving their legs. The natural look extended to clothing, too. Both men and women wore handmade or natural fiber clothing, or no clothes at all. Nudist colonies and nude beaches flourished, and at concerts and festivals women often doffed their tops. Those who weren't quite uninhibited enough to forgo clothing altogether limited their nudity to their feet.

Peasant blouses, gypsy skirts, Nehru jackets, and dashikis

Hippie mother and child, 1971

PHOTO BY VIC FAHRER

Most frustrating to the confused older generation was the unisex, or androgynous, look. With girls in short hair and boys in ponytails, both wearing jeans and T-shirts, old folks couldn't tell one sex from the other, and that, they thought, was going a bit too far.

FRANK, a rock and roll band, Athens, Georgia, 1969

Silk Road Halter Top

*i*n the '60s, girls tied blue and white bandanas into halter tops for cheap chic. This updated version instead uses a beautiful silk paisley scarf for bohemian elegance.

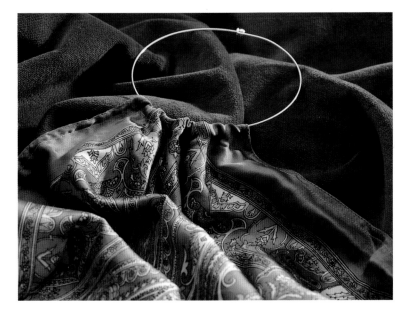

You Will Need

Scarf, approximately 36 inches (91.4 cm) square*

Sewing machine

Metal choker necklace

Straight pins

Matching thread

*Your scarf must be a square and it must be large enough, when folded, to go around your waist and tie in a knot.

1 Fold the scarf, making a triangle.

2 Starting at the top point, machine-stitch very close to the edge down one side of the scarf. Turn the scarf over and stitch down the other side. Be sure to catch both sides of the scarf in the stitches.

3 Fold the top point of the triangle about 3 inches (7.6 cm) over the metal necklace and pin in place.

4 Stitch the folded point about 1/2 inch (1.3 cm) from the necklace. The necklace can be removed for washing.

5 To wear the halter, just fold up the bottom long edge to a place that you're comfortable with, then tie the two free ends in a knot behind your back.

Designer: *Kathryn Temple*

Patchwork Purse

*a*nother innovative use for an old pair of jeans. The contrasting colors of denim add interest, and the beaded butterfly patch dresses it up a bit.

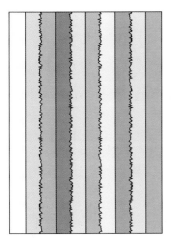

Figure 1

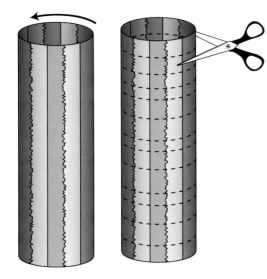

Figure 2   **Figure 3**

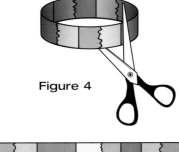

Figure 4

Figure 5

1. Cut out 10 strips of denim, each 30 inches (76.2 cm) long and 2 to 3 inches (5.1 to 7.3 cm) wide.

2. Sew the strips together lengthwise. Sew some strips so that the raw edges face the back and leave the raw edges exposed on others (figure 1). Continue until all of the strips have been sewn together into a rectangle.

3. Sew the two 30-inch-long (76.2 cm) edges together so that you have a "tube" of fabric (figure 2).

4. Cut across the tube to create "circles" of fabric. Vary the height of the sections from 2 to 4 inches (5.1 to 10.2 cm) (figure 3).

5. Turn the circles back into strips by cutting them at varying points. If you cut the circle on a dark denim square for one, for example, cut the next circle on a lighter denim square (figure 4). This is important so that when you line these pieces back up they will fall into a random patchwork design.

6. Now, sew the strips together. Treat them just as you did the original strips of fabric in step 2. You should now have a 14 x 24-inch (35.5 x 61 cm) patchwork rectangle (figure 5).

7. Sew a 1/2-inch (1.3 cm) hem on each of the 14-inch (35.5 cm) edges.

8. Next, fold the rectangle in half so that the finished surface of the fabric faces inward and the "rough" side faces out.

9. Sew the two sides together.

10. Keeping the purse inside out, locate one of the bottom corners of the purse. Pinch the fabric on each side of the corner and pull (figures 6 and 7). Use a straight pin to hold the corner in this flattened position and sew a 2-inch (5.1 cm) seam.

11. Repeat step 10 on the other side.

You Will Need

Scissors

2 pairs of old blue jeans

Sewing machine

Blue thread

Straight pins

Large safety pin

6-inch (14.6 cm) piece of string

Wooden bead

10-inch (25.4 cm) piece of leather cord

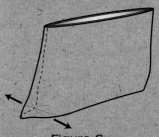

Figure 6

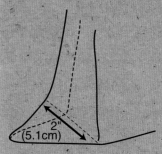

2" (5.1cm)

Figure 7

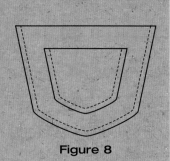

Figure 8

12 Set the purse aside for a moment and cut out the back pocket and surrounding fabric of the jeans. Include plenty of fabric above the opening of the pocket (figure 8).

13 Sew a hem along the sides of the back pocket so that it is approximately the same width as your purse.

14 Next, hem the edges below the pocket so they form a point.

15 Keeping the purse inside out, use straight pins to secure the raw edge of the pocket along the inside lip of the purse. Sew it into place.

16 Cut a long strip of denim for your strap. Make sure it is at least 4 inches (10.2 cm) wide. Fold it so that the finished side is facing in, then sew along the seam.

17 Pin the large safety pin the one edge of the strap and use it to "fish" the end back through the strap. Continue inching it along until you have flipped it inside out and the "finished" side is exposed.

18 Use straight pins to fasten the strap to the inside edges of the sides of the purse and sew them into place.

19 Thread the piece of string through the wooden bead and tie a knot at the back center of the bead. Knot the string tightly, then sew the knot to the purse.

20 Sew a loop of leather cord onto the inner edge of the purse flap. Use the loop to fasten the bead and keep the purse closed.

You Will Need

Fabric pen

Template on page 143

Yellow ribbon, 1-inch (2.5 cm) thick

Scissors

Straight pins

Needle and matching thread

Beading needle

Beading thread

Seed beads

For the Butterfly Patch

1 With the fabric pen, trace the template onto the ribbon and cut out the two upper wings and two lower wings.

2 Use the straight pins to attach the wings to the pocket of the purse.

3 Using a continuous loop stitch, sew the wings onto the pocket. Make sure you sew through only the top layer of the pocket.

4 Using the beading needle and thread, sew the body of the butterfly onto the pocket. String four or five beads onto the thread, and then stitch them onto the butterfly body. Pass the needle back through the pocket, then loop back through one or two of the previously sewn beads. Add four or five more beads and repeat.

5 Sew symmetrical patterns of beads onto the wings, using the same method described in step 4.

YESTERDAY'S PATCHWORK

Jeans skirts by Bea Slater

PHOTO COURTESY OF JEAN RAY LAURY AND JOYCE AIKEN

INSET PHOTO COURTESY OF
ALEXANDRA JACOPETTI HART AND THE
ESTATE OF JERRY WAINWRIGHT

Jeans Patches

Designer: *Kathryn Temple*

according to hippie philosophy, a worn area in a pair of jeans doesn't mean they're ready for the trash: It means they're ready for a patch. These two classic hippie symbols are the perfect choice for adding flower power to your jeans.

For the Flower Patch

1 With the fabric pen, trace the petal template onto a piece of fabric and cut out the shape.

2 Trace the circle onto a contrasting piece of fabric and cut it out.

3 Sew the circle onto the petals, using a continuous loop stitch. Try to get the stitches close together for durability.

4 Use straight pins to position the patch over the rip in the jeans. Use the same stitch as above to stitch the petals onto the jeans.

For the Peace Symbol Patch

1 With the fabric pen, trace the peace symbol template onto a bandana and cut out the shape.

2 Apply an even amount of fabric glue to the back of the peace symbol and press it firmly into place on the jeans.

3 Allow to dry overnight before wearing.

You Will Need

Fabric pen

Templates on page 143

Fabric in different patterns and colors or bandanas

Scissors

Needle and thick thread

Straight pins

Fabric glue (for peace symbol patch)

Stop Children, What's That Sound

Less than a decade after Elvis Presley's sexy dancing had shocked the world, his moves seemed positively chaste in comparison to the far-out fashion, provocative lyrics, and tripped-out grooves that came to characterize rock music by 1965. Across the musical spectrum, rock, folk, and even pop music began to reflect the seismic cultural shifts taking place on all levels of society in North America and in Europe. Previously taboo topics, such as sex and drugs, were no longer off limits, and protest songs became touchstones of the antiwar movement.

Folk music had evolved from cheerful ditties and earnest ballads of the folk revival of the late '50s into a powerful tool for political protest and social activism. Bob Dylan hit the folk scene in 1962, and touched a cultural nerve with songs like "Blowin'

Tom Pitman, founder of the Austin Lounge Lizards , 1968

Sparky Rucker at the Smoke Festival of the Folkies, 1972 PHOTO BY SHARON FAHRER

in the Wind," "The Times They are A-Changin'," and "Hard Rain is A-Gonna Fall." The Newport Folk Festival in 1963 made stars of Dylan and Joan Baez, and spawned a whole new generation of folk singers. Simon and Garfunkel invented the folk pop sound, and when folk went electric, bands such as the Byrds and The Mamas and The Papas invented folk rock, a combination of folky lyrics and jangly guitars and synthesizers. Country Joe and the Fish fused protest lyrics with rock in songs such as, "Fixin' to Die Rag," which became the anthem of the antiwar movement.

Stones were influenced by the Beatles to some extent, and in turn, they influenced new streams of musical experiment. There was the blues-influenced rock genre,

even the Rolling Stones were influenced by the Beatles

The Rolling Stones and Chuck Berry in concert, 1969
PHOTOS BY DANA IRWIN

with stars such as Big Brother and the Holding Company, featuring Janis Joplin; the psychedelic pop-rock sound of bands such as The Strawberry Alarm Clock ("Incense and Peppermint"), the Lemon Pipers ("Green Tambourine"), Donovan ("Mellow Yellow"), and the Troggs ("Wild Thing"); and acid rock, a heavier sound developed by Jimi Hendrix and bands like Steppenwolf ("Born to Be Wild" and "Magic Carpet Ride") and Cream ("White Room").

Donovan, 1970
PHOTO BY DANA IRWIN

Ever the innovators, the Beatles transformed rock music with their Sgt. Pepper's Lonely Heart's Club Band in 1967, an album which introduced new forms of composition (such as the introduction of the sitar to rock music) and lyrics, paving the way for what became known as psychedelic rock. The Doors, Jefferson Airplane, and even the Rolling

For the youth of the '60s, music wasn't just a form of entertainment. It gave voice to their fears and provided a forum for articulating their vision of the future. It helped them to express their new-found sense of artistic and sexual freedom. It provided a cool soundtrack for tripping out and experimenting with drugs. But most of all, music brought people together. At protest rallies, thousands of people sang together for peace. At the Woodstock and Monterey festivals (the biggest events of the hippie era), tens of thousands of hippies grooved together to prove that peace, love, and harmony really were attainable ideals, if only for a short while.

Joan Baez © AP/WIDE WORLD PHOTO

Summer in the city,
dressin' so fine and looking so pretty

Tie-Dye and Batik

s there any craft more strongly identified with hippies than tie-dye? The bright colors and swirling patterns were a favorite with trippy hippies and hippie wannabes. Tie-dyed T-shirts, pants, and dresses were the staple of any hippie wardrobe, and many a hippie pad was decorated with tie-dyed bed sheets, curtains, wall hangings, and pillows. Batik was all the rage, too. From dashikis to sarongs and capes, batik clothing captured the spirit of the ethnic look hippies craved.

Fast forward to today, and tie-dye and batik clothing and housewares are still in demand. You can still get a far-out T-shirt from the back of a van at a concert, but tie-dye and batik have now made it into the mainstream, too. Today's color palette is a little more subtle, and the patterns are a little less psychedelic, but the technique is just as creative as ever. The projects in this section offer new approaches to the craft—a different type of tie-dyed T-shirt, a shibori (Japanese tie-dye) shawl, and a batik pillow cover in a rich new palette.

Big photo: John Sebastian of the Lovin' Spoonful wearing tie-dye. © HENRY DILTZ/CORBIS *Second photo, Dress by Joyce Aiken. Fourth photo, shirt by Elizabeth Fuller.*

Today's Tie-Dye

Designer: MARY PEREZ

Brightly colored tie-dyed T-shirts in psychedelic patterns were *the* cornerstone of hippie fashion. Today they've made it into the mainstream and can be found in colors, patterns, and styles to suit every taste. If you haven't learned to do tie-dye yet, here's your chance.

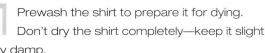

1 Prewash the shirt to prepare it for dying. Don't dry the shirt completely—keep it slightly damp.

2 Accordion pleat the shirt, starting from one shoulder and moving down. Keep your folds tight for a tight pattern (figure 1).

3 With the string or rubber bands, bind the pleated shirt tightly, about every 1 inch (2.5 cm).

4 In the buckets, prepare your dyes according to the manufacturer's instructions.

5 Use an eye dropper or plastic bottle to apply the dye to the shirt, alternating the rows of colors (figure 2).

6 Put the shirt in a plastic bag and let it sit for 24 hours.

7 Rinse the shirt according to the dye manufacturer's instructions, and let it dry.

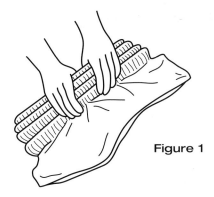

Figure 1

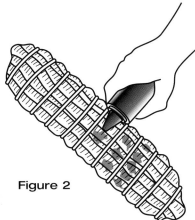

Figure 2

YOU WILL NEED

100% cotton shirt (preferably white, ribbed texture)

String or rubber bands

2 buckets

Fiber reactive dyes in two shades*

Eye dropper or plastic bottle

Plastic bag

*Available at craft stores

YESTERDAY'S TIE-DYE
Shirts by Joyce Aiken
PHOTO COURTESY OF JOYCE AIKEN

FREE YOUR MIND

Those seeking a high without the drugs looked to the East for spiritual enlightenment. During the '60s, interest in Eastern religion, meditation, and alternative religions grew dramatically among middle class European and North American youth. Young people went to India in droves, taking up residence in the ever-growing number of ashrams (spiritual retreat centers).

The Beat writers and poets (who had started so many trends that eventually trickled down to the hippies) were the first to introduce Eastern philosophy to the young generation. Jack Kerouac's *The Dharma Bums* (Viking Press, 1958) acquainted readers with the tenets of Buddhism, and Allen Ginsberg's live performances featured Vedic chanting, a Hindu practice of repeating the same sound outwardly to lead to harmony in mind, body, and spirit.

The Beatles join Maharishi Mahesh Yogi in Wales for a week of meditation.
© AP/WIDE WORLD PHOTO

In 1967, the Beatles began to follow Maharishi Mahesh Yogi, a guru who advocated Transcendental Mediation, a belief system aimed at achieving greater consciousness through meditation and yoga. Although it was based on ancient Hindu texts, TM was a new interpretation that wasn't exactly Hindu and was considered a fad religion by its detractors. But the Beatles' endorsement of the practice led millions to follow the Maharishi, and inspired others to take up meditation and yoga or other avenues to inner peace.

Interest in Native American spiritual rituals grew as well. Age-old tribal rituals, such as the vision quest (a trek into the wilderness to seek clarity), were co-opted by hippies looking for higher consciousness. Aldous Huxley's 1954 novel *Doors of Perception* (Chatto and Windus) described the heightened awarness he felt after taking mescaline, a hallucinogenic substance derived from the peyote cactus. Carlos Casteneda, an anthropologist of sorts, became a kind of guru of mystical experiences when he published his arguably fictional stories about mescaline-induced experiences with a Mexican shaman.

New religions (some of which are now considered to have been cults) were formed and often quickly disbanded during the hippie years. Some grew rapidly and continued to recruit new members, such as the International Society for

The Beat writers and poets were the first to introduce Eastern philosophy to the young generation.

Krishna Consciousness, or Hare Krishna, which was founded in 1966 and still exists today. In other cases, the spiritual leader of a group was nothing more than a con man out for personal gain. Many cults employed what became known as mind-control techniques to ensure the devotion of their members. Vulnerable young people (many of whom were hooked on drugs) fell in with such groups until their families came to get them and "deprogram" them.

Fueled by a collective interest in self-knowledge and understanding, astrology became popular in the late '60s, and the now cliché line "What's your sign?" came into currency. The Age of Aquarius, hailed by astrologers as a new era that would bring freedom, was said to have started in 1965. In hippie gathering places, one could always find someone to read a chart or even an aura.

The spiritual searching that characterized the '60s gradually gave way to the materialism that has become synonymous with the '80s. But those years left their mark. Concepts and practices such as yoga and astrology, which once seemed outlandish, are now an accepted feature of the cultural landscape.

Designer: **Lynne Caldwell**

Shibori Shawl

Shibori is the traditional Japanese form of tie-dying, typically done by wrapping a piece of cloth around a pole or pipe, then tying it off. The procedure used for this shawl is a little less labor-intensive than traditional shibori, so it's fun to experiment with.

YOU WILL NEED

2 yards (1.8 m) of silk fabric, pre-dyed

Uncooked popcorn kernels

Cotton string, about 3 yards (2.7 m)

Green fiber-reactive dye*

Bucket or sink for dye vat

Scissors

Iron

Feather embellish-ments*

Needle and thread

*Available at craft stores

Note: This material can be handwashed or dry-cleaned.

1 Pinch a small area of the silk and place an unpopped piece of popcorn into the fold created in your hand. Tie a piece of cotton string around the fabric and popcorn. To create patterns of different sizes, wrap the kernel just once in some places for small circles and several times in others for larger circles. Repeat this process for as many patterns as you want to see, closer or farther apart, depending on your preference.

2 Following the manufacturer's instructions, prepare the dye in a bucket and overdye the fabric. The areas that you have tied off will remain in the original color and the rest of the piece will reflect the overdye.

3 After the fabric has dried, clip off all of the cotton yarn, remove the popcorn, and iron the fabric.

4 Fold the fabric in half and sew the short ends together to create a substantial shawl.

5 Hand-sew the feather embellishments to the short edges of the shawl.

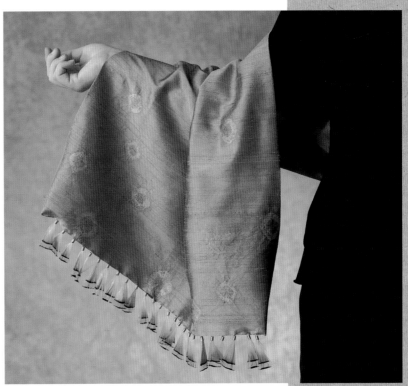

Surrealistic Pillow

Designer: Lynne Caldwell

Try some ethnic accents, such as this batik pillow, for a subtle way to add a bohemian touch to your decor. Batik is a wonderful medium for self-expression—you can make freeform designs improvisationally. You can easily find the materials you need at craft stores, and because there are no rules, the pattern you create is up to you.

1 Following the manufacturer's instructions, prepare the yellow dye in one of the buckets and dye the white cotton fabric.

2 Next, you'll need to prepare the wax for the batik. You have a few options in terms of the wax you use. Beeswax is very elastic and doesn't crack much. Paraffin wax cracks a lot (which results in a lot of the color "veins" you see in batik). Blending the two waxes will get you a nice consistency, but you could also just use beeswax on its own. If you do mix the waxes, put an equal amount of each into your double boiler. Allow the wax to melt, but don't let it get much hotter than that (Use your thermometer to make sure it doesn't get above 250 to 300°F [121 to 148°C]).

3 Use the tjanting tool to apply the melted wax to the areas that you want to remain yellow.

4 Following the manufacturer's instructions, prepare the wine-colored dye in a bucket or in the sink, and dye the fabric. Leave the fabric in the dye vat for about 20 minutes, then remove it and let it dry.

5 Repeat the process of dying the fabric with the wine-colored dye three more times. Each time, leave the fabric in the dye vat for a longer period of time until you reach 1 hour. Let the fabric dry.

6 Removed the wax by placing absorbent paper over the wax and ironing it with a warm iron. Do this on both sides of the fabric.

7 If you want more embellishments, sew beads around the edge of the batik using fishing line at three-stitch intervals.

You Will Need

Yellow fiber-reactive dye*

2 buckets or sink for dye vat

White cotton fabric

Beeswax, 1/2 to 3/4 pound (227 to 340 g)*

Paraffin wax (optional)**

Double boiler

Candy or candlemaking thermometer*

Tjanting tool*

Wine-colored fiber-reactive dye*

Newsprint or other absorbent paper

Iron

Beading needle (optional)

Beading thread or fishing line (optional)

Medium to large-sized beads (optional)

*Available at craft stores

**Available at grocery stores

Note: Batik items should be cleaned in cold water.

Who Are You?

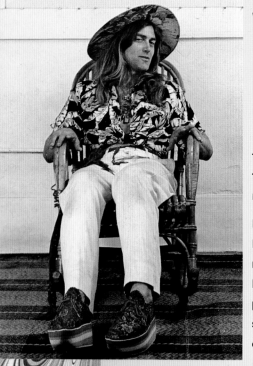

A guy called Apple Cobbler
PHOTO COURTESY OF ALEXANDRA JACOPETTI HART AND THE ESTATE OF JERRY WAINWRIGHT

Young men and women who had grown up in the '50s as "Betty" and "Jim" found a way to rebel and express their new hippie identity: by changing their names. Some did it legally, some just adopted a new name for a short time, some went through several names and identities, and others kept their names but resolved to give their children ones more in line with the times.

Hippie names tended to fall into several categories. Perhaps the most popular were names taken from nature. River, Rain, Rainbow, Star, Skye, Sunshine, Butterfly, Dove, and Sage are some of the names hippies took for themselves or gave to their children. The singer Jewel is an example of the "my parents were hippies" syndrome, as are the famously named Moon Unit Zappa and the actress Soliel Moon Frye. Seasonal names such as Summer or Autumn were also big, as were names with a cosmic ring to them, such as Celeste, Ariel, Aurora, and Luna.

Katia, aka Sky

Another category of hippie names was inspired by the Eastern religious and mystic experiences hippies were having. India was a popular name for girls, as was Karma, Dharma, Chakra, and Shiva, while Krishna and Vishnu were big names for boys. Michelle and John Phillips of The Mamas and The Papas called one daughter Chyna and the other Bijoux. Often a new name was bestowed upon a person by his or her guru or shaman. Dick Alpert, Timothy Leary's fellow LSD researcher at Harvard, was given the name Ram Dass ("servant of God") by his guru, and he still goes by it today.

Other names echoed the hippie philosophy of peace, love, and freedom. Destiny, Harmony, Love, Melody, and Shalom were some of the selections in this category.

Hippies also honored their favorite musicians by giving their children names such as Dylan, Lennon, Janis, Jerry (or Garcia), and Donovan. Then there were those who honored their favorite drug by naming themselves or their daughters Mary Jane or Maria Juana.

Those who discovered Native American culture and spirituality often changed their names to reflect its practice of using animal and spirit names. Silver Wolf, White Elk, Climbing Sun, Singing Hawk, Rain Dancer, and Coyote are some examples.

African Americans got into the name-change game by relinquishing their "slave names" and replacing their last names with X, as Malcolm X had done. Others chose to adopt something that sounded African—the Beat poet Leroi Jones changed his name to Amiri Baraka. Those who converted to Islam chose a new Islamic name to reflect their spiritual rebirth. H. Rapp Brown, a leader of the Student Nonviolent Coordinating Committee, became Jamil Abdullah Al Amin, and the boxer Cassius Clay became Mohammed Ali.

Although the '80s brought a backlash in free-spirited names and a rash of children with blue-blood names such as Amanda and Bradford, there seems to be a resurgence of hippie names. In any given kindergarten class today you can find Dakotas and Dylans playing happily.

Wavy Gravy © BETTMAN/CORBIS

River, Rain, Rainbow, Star, Skye, Sunshine

A woman named Carnation
PHOTO COURTESY OF ALEXANDRA JACOPETTI HART AND THE ESTATE OF JERRY WAINWRIGHT

GET YOUR MOTOR RUNNING HEAD OUT ON THE HIGHWAY

Photos left to right: Cape by Judith Weston, photo courtesy of Alexandra Jacopetti Hart and the Estate of Jerry Wainwright; crochet dress by Chrstina Luell, photo courtesy of Jean Ray Laury and Joyce Aiken.

Newlyweds on mortorcycle © BETTMAN/CORBIS

CROCHET

Prior to the '60s, crochet was strongly associated with grandmothers. The very word brought to mind doilies and frilly baby clothes. In other words, it was square. But street market crafters revived the tradition, reinterpreting the time-honored craft in far-out, groovy new ways. Creative patterns and bold color combinations made for cutting-edge crochet. Soon the fashion houses in New York and Paris took notice, and they started creating crochet designs of their own. Crochet hats, vests, purses, ponchos, and dresses were must-haves for the hippie wardrobe, and every hippie home had a granny square afghan. With a nod to their hippie roots, but a fresh color palette, the designs in this section of the book are wonderful, wearable, and easy to make. If you need a refresher course on crochet abbreviations and stitches, see the reference section on page 140.

Designer: **JANE DAVIS**

HOMESTEAD SHAWL

for comfort and style, you can't beat a "spiderweb" shawl, a classic hippie design with earthy appeal. The variegated yarn used in this version gives the shawl distinction and sophistication, too.

Skill Level

Intermediate

Finished Size

Approximately 33 x 66 inches (83.8 cm x 1.6 m) from center top to center bottom point

Body of Shawl

Foundation: Beginning at the center bottom point, ch 9, sl st in 1st st to join into a circle, do not turn.

Row 1: Ch 7, sc in circle, ch 5, dc in circle, turn.

Row 2: Ch 7, sc in first lp, ch 5, sc in next lp, ch 5, dc in same lp, turn.

Row 3: Ch 7, sc in first lp, [ch 5, sc in next lp], repeat to the end, ch 5, dc in last lp again, turn.

Rows 4 to 58: Repeat row 3. Do not turn at the end of row 58, but continue down the side with edging.

Edging

Row 1: Ch 3, 2 dc in first lp, [ch 1, 2 dc in next lp] repeat along one side of shawl to center point, [ch 1, 2 dc, ch 3, 2 dc] in lp of center point, [ch 1, 2 dc in next lp] repeat along second side of shawl, ending with 3 dc in last lp, turn.

Row 2: Ch 2, [ch 3, dc] three times in ea ch sp along the side, then six times in the center bottom ch sp, then three times in ea ch sp along the next side, ch 5, sl st in corner of shawl. Cut yarn and weave in ends.

Steam press the body of the shawl, stretching it slightly to the finished measurements. Do not press the ruffled edge.

This project was made using two skeins (each 175 yards [157 m]) of Reynolds Yarns Harmony 4-ounce (113 g) 100% wool yarn in medium green #9.

YOU WILL NEED

2 skeins (each 172 yards [157 m]) of variegated worsted-weight yarn in green

Size I hook

Scissors

Large tapestry needle

Iron

Abbreviations

See page 140

Gauge

4 sts = 1 inch (2,5 cm)

Stitches Used

ch

sc

dc

Designer: **JANE DAVIS**

VIOLET SKYE HAT

a soft and cozy topper for a free-spirited hippie look, this hat is easy to make and looks good on just about everyone.

Skill Level

Easy

Finished Size

22-inch (5.6 cm) circumference

Pattern Notes and Special Stitches

Beginning chs in rows and count as a st.

Do not turn at the end of rows after foundation.

2-dc cluster: Yo, insert hk in st, yo, pull through st, yo, pull through 2 lps on hk, yo, insert hk in same st, yo, pull through st, yo, pull through 2 lps on hk, yo, pull through all lps on hk.

3-dc cluster: Yo, insert hk in st, yo, pull through st, yo, pull through 2 lps on hk, (yo, insert hk in same st, yo, pull through st, yo, pull through 2 lps on hk) twice, yo, pull through all lps on hk.

4-dc cluster: Yo, insert hk in st, yo, pull through st, yo, pull through 2 lps on hk, (yo, insert hk in same st, yo, pull through st, yo, pull through 2 lps on hk) three times, yo, pull through all lps on hk.

Foundation: Ch 4, turn.

Round 1: 15 sc in 4th ch from hk, sl st in top of ch 4 (16 sts).

Round 2: Ch 3, 2 dc in next st, (dc in next st, 2 dc in next st) 7 times, sl st in top of ch-3 (24 sts).

Round 3: Ch 3, dc in next st, 2 dc in next st, (dc in next 2 sts, 2 dc in next st) 7 times, sl st in top of ch-3 (32 sts).

Round 4: Ch 3, dc in next 2 sts, 2 dc in next st, (dc in next 3 sts, 2 dc in next st) 7 times, sl st in top of ch-3 (40 sts).

Round 5: Ch 3, dc in next 3 sts, 2 dc in next st, (dc in next 4 sts, 2 dc in next st) 7 times, sl st in top of ch-3 (48 sts).

Round 6: Ch 3, dc in next 4 sts, 2 dc in next st, (dc in next 5 sts, 2 dc in next st) 7 times, sl st in top of ch-3 (56 sts).

Round 7: Ch 3, dc in next 5 sts, 2 dc in next st, (dc in next 6 sts, 2 dc in next st) 7 times, sl st in top of ch-3 (64 sts).

Round 8: Ch 3, dc in next 6 sts, 2 dc in next st, (dc in next 7 sts, 2 dc in next st) 7 times, sl st in top of ch-3 (72 sts).

Round 9: Ch 3, dc in next 7 sts, 2 dc in next st, (dc in next 8 sts, 2 dc in next st) 7 times, sl st in top of ch-3 (80 sts).

Round 10: Ch 3, 2-st cluster in 1st st, ch 1, sk next st, (3-dc cluster in next st, ch 1, sk next st) repeat around, sl st in top of ch-3.

Round 11: Ch 4, 4-dc cluster in next ch sp, (ch 1, dc in next ch sp, ch 1, 4-dc cluster in next ch sp) repeat around, ch 1 sl st in 3rd ch of ch-4.

Round 12: Ch 3, 2-dc cluster in 1st ch sp, ch 1, (3-dc cluster in next ch sp, ch 1) repeat around, sl st in top of ch-3.

Round 13: Ch 3, dc in 1st st, (2 dc in next ch sp) repeat around, sl st in top of ch-3.

Rounds 14 and 15: Ch 3, dc in ea st around, sl st in top of ch-3.

Round 16: Ch 1, sc in ea st around. Cut yarn and weave in ends.

The sample project was made using one skein (218 yards [199 m]) of Knit One Crochet Two's Parfait Solids worsted-weight 3.5-ounce (100 g) 100% cotton yarn in eggplant #1730.

YOU WILL NEED

1 skein of 3.5 oz. (100 g) worsted-weight yarn in eggplant

Size H crochet hook

Scissors

Large tapestry needle

Abbreviations

See page 140

Gauge in double crochet

15 sts = 4 inches (10.2 cm)

8 rows = 4 inches (10.2 cm)

Stitches Used

ch

2-dc

3-dc

4-dc

FEED YOUR HEAD (and Your Body)

In the '50s, modern technology transformed the work of the middle-class housewife, offering her new inventions to lighten her workload. To revolutionize her duties in the kitchen, she was offered prepared foods—frozen, canned, boxed, and full of chemicals, preservatives, and artificial flavors.

Hippies rejected processed food like every other aspect of their parents' value system. Their desire for all things natural extended to what they ate, leading them to seek out alternatives to the conventional diets they had grown up with.

While spaghetti and meatballs had been the most exotic ethnic food available in the '50s, the increased interest in Indian and Asian spirituality helped spur an interest in the cuisine of those cultures, too. Middle Eastern foods (such as humus and tahini) were rediscovered by hippies in their travels, and Mexican and Central American food, once considered "peasant food," gained new cachet.

Vegetarianism, which was considered by doctors to be unhealthy well into the '60s, became more popular. Vegetarian restaurants started to appear in hippie-friendly areas. Many began to advocate the macrobiotic philosophy, brought to the United States by a Japanese scientist in the late '50s. The macrobiotic diet features unrefined foods (such as brown rice and whole grains); vegetables grown organically and locally and eaten in season; sea vegetables, such as seaweed, and no milk or animal products.

PHOTO COURTESY OF ALEXANDRA JACOPETTI HART
& THE ESTATE OF JERRY WAINWRIGHT

Hippie communes discovered the soybean, which had been a staple of the Asian diet for centuries. The Farm, a commune in Tennessee, published one of the first vegetarian cookbooks, featuring recipes that included tofu, soymilk, and other nondairy products.

In hippie-friendly communities, grocery co-ops started to appear in the late '60s, offering staple products in bulk to reduce price and packaging, organic produce (usually locally grown), fresh whole grain breads, and bean sprouts. Health food stores, later called natural food stores, came along a few years down the road. At first, many of the stores were poorly stocked: The dusty shelves housed only a selection of herbal supplements and some jars of wheat germ. The proprietors generally weren't very business savvy, and some were even averse to the idea of making money and being part of the establishment. As time went by, though, what had been a few local stores here and there turned into a natural foods industry, offering all sorts of wholesome foods, from tamari to tempeh to rice cakes.

And what about granola, the food most famously associated with hippies? It was actually developed in the 1880s by Sylvester Graham, inventor of the graham cracker and Corn Flakes breakfast cereal. An avid proponent of vegetarianism and abstention from alcohol, tobacco, and caffeine, Graham broke up some graham crackers, and called it Granula. Later, his rival, Dr. Kellogg of cereal fame, added dried fruit, nuts, and honey to the mix, renamed it Granola, and marketed it as a breakfast cereal. Granola caught on with hippies because it was all natural.

 MANY BEGAN TO ADVOCATE THE MACROBIOTIC PHILOSOPHY

Woman baking bread at The Group Commune, Arkansas, 1971

MOTHER EARTH NEWS, www.motherearthnews.com

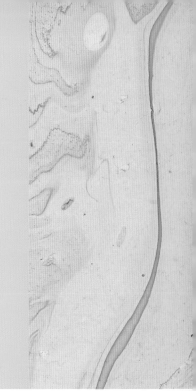

Designer: JANE DAVIS

AQUARIUS AMULET BAG

this tiny bag is like a lovely piece of crochet jewelry that's decorative and easy to make.

Skill Level

Easy

Finished Size

Approximately 2 inches (5 cm) wide by 2½ inches (6.4 cm) tall, not including strap

Pattern Notes

Hold one strand of ea crochet cotton cord together as one throughout.

The whole bag is made in one piece, beginning with the body of the bag, then connecting the sides, then making the strap.

Foundation: Ch 11, turn.

Row 1: Ch 1, sc in 2nd ch from hk and ea ch across, turn.

Rows 2 to 30: Ch 1, sc in ea st across, turn. At the end of row 30, do not cut.

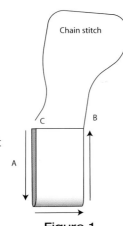

Chain stitch

Figure 1

To form the bag, fold the crochetwork in half so the first and last rows meet. Continuing from the last st in row 30 starting at A (figure 1), work through both layers along the side of the folded piece. Sc through both layers along one side, work 3 sc in the corner, then sc along the bottom, 3 sc in the corner, then sc up the other side of the piece. You now have a bag shape. Now, starting at B (figure 1), make the strap your desired length by making chain stitches. Sl st in the other corner of the bag, then sl st one st away along the edge of the bag (C in figure 1), turn and sc in ea ch along the strap until you reach the other corner of the bag. Cut and weave in ends.

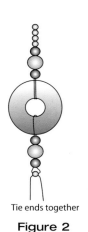

Tie ends together

Figure 2

Adding the Beads

Thread one strand of crochet cotton and pull it through the eye of the needle so it's a double strand. Attach the thread to the center back opening of the bag. String the beads in the following order: three small wooden beads, one bronze bead, one large wooden bead, one bronze bead. Pass the thread through the doughnut and back through the beads. Knot the thread to the back of the bag. Cut and weave in the ends.

Cut a 6-inch (15.2 cm) piece of crochet cotton cord. String one small wooden bead, one bronze bead, one large wooden bead and one bronze bead. Pass through the doughnut, then back through all the beads except the small wooden bead. Pass through the small wooden bead in the opposite direction. Each end of the cord will be coming out the opposite hole (figure 2). Tie the ends in a square knot. Cut to ¼ inch (6 mm) long.

The sample project was made using one ball (each 284 yards [260 m]) of DMC's Cebelia size 10 1¾-ounce (50 g) 100% cotton yarn in both oatmeal and tan.

YOU WILL NEED

1 ball each of size 10 crochet cotton cord in both oatmeal and tan

Size D crochet hook

Scissors

Tapestry needle small enough to pass through all the beads with an eye large enough to thread with the crochet cotton cord

4 small (about 3/16-inch [5 mm] diameter) wooden beads

4 bronze-colored beads, size 5

2 large (about ¼-inch [6 mm] diameter) wooden beads

Doughnut bead, 1 to ¼-inch (2.5 to 3.1 cm) wide

Abbreviations

See page 140

Gauge

24 sts = 4 inches (10.2 cm)

26 rows = 4 inches (10.2 cm)

Stitches Used

ch

sl st

sc

Designer: JANE DAVIS

FEELIN' GROOVY VEST

*t*his feminine and easygoing vest has style that spans the decades. In terms of skill, it's a little more complicated than some of the other projects in this section, but the result is definitely worth the effort.

Skill Level

Intermediate

Finished Size

Chest: 40 inches (102 cm) (44 inches [112 cm], 48 inches [122 cm])

Length: 24 inches (61 cm) (25 inches [64 cm], 26 inches [66 cm])

Pattern Notes

Body pattern: Ch 5, 2 dc in 1st ch sp, (ch 2, 2 dc in next ch sp) repeat across.

In row 2, the ch-3 is not counted as a stitch, and the chain at the end of row 1 is counted as a stitch.

When decreasing, if you ch 3 at the beg of a row, or dc in a ch sp without making a ch-2 first, you no longer work into those spaces on the next row.

Back

Foundation, Bottom edge of back: Ch 94 (102, 109), turn.

Row 1: Ch 3, dc in the 4th ch from hk and ea ch across, turn 94 (102, 109) sts.

Row 2: Ch 5, sk next st, dc in next st, ch 2, sk next 2 sts, dc in next st (ch 2, sk next st, dc in next st, ch 2, sk next 2 sts, dc in next st) 18 (19, 21) times, (for medium size only: ch 2, sk next 2 sts, dc in next st), turn 38 (41, 44) repeats.

Rows 3 to 29 (31, 33): Ch 5, dc in next ch sp, (ch 2, dc in next ch sp) repeat across, turn.

Row 30 (32, 34): Armhole shaping: Sl st across the first 3 ch sps, ch 3, dc in next ch sp, (ch 2, dc in next ch sp) repeat to last 4 ch sps, dc in next ch sp, turn, 30 (33, 36) repeats.

Row 31 (33, 35): Ch 3, dc in first ch sp, (ch 2, dc in next ch sp) repeat to last ch sp, dc in last ch sp, turn, 28 (31, 34) repeats.

Rows 32 (34, 36) to 56 (58, 60): Work even in patt.

Row 57 (59, 61): Neckline shaping: Work in patt across first 8 (10, 11) patt repeats, weave in end. Attach a new yarn at the 8th (10th, 11th) ch sp from the other end and work 8 (10, 11) patt repeats.

Right Front

Foundation: Ch 47 (52, 55), turn.

Row 1: Ch 3, dc in the 4th ch from hk and ea ch across, turn 47 (52, 55) sts.

Row 2: Ch 5, sk next st, dc in next st (ch 2, sk next 2 sts, dc in next st, ch 2, sk next st, dc in next st) 9 (10, 10) times, (for largest size only: ch 2, sk next 2 sts, dc in next st), turn 19 (21, 23) repeats.

Rows 3 to 29 (31, 33): Ch 5, dc in 1st ch sp, (ch 2, dc in next ch sp) repeat across, turn.

Row 30 (32, 34): Sl st across first 3 ch sps, ch 3, dc in next ch sp, (ch 2, dc in next ch sp) repeat across, turn.

Row 31 (33, 35): Work in patt to last ch sp, dc in last ch sp, turn.

Row 32 (34, 36): Ch 5, dc in 1st ch sp, (ch 2, dc in next ch sp) repeat across, turn.

Rows 33 (35, 37) to 57 (59, 61): Work even on armhole side and decrease one patt rep on center front every other row, 5 times, then work even through last row.

Left Front

Foundation: Ch 47 (52, 55), turn.

Row 1: Ch 3, dc in the 4th ch from hk and ea ch across, turn 47 (52, 55) sts.

Row 2: Ch 5, sk next st, dc in next st, (ch 2, sk next 2 sts, dc in next st, ch 2, sk next st, dc in next st) 9 (10, 10) times. For largest size only: ch 2, sk next 2 sts, dc in next st), turn 19 (21, 23) repeats.

Rows 3 to 30 (32, 34): Ch 5, dc in 1st ch sp, (ch 2, dc in next ch sp) repeat across, turn.

Row 31 (33, 35): Sl st across first 3 ch sps, ch 3, dc in next ch sp (ch 2, dc in next ch sp) repeat across, turn.

Row 32 (34, 36): Work in patt to last ch sp, dc in last ch sp, turn.

Row 33 (35, 37): Ch 5, dc in 1st ch sp, (ch 2, dc in next ch sp) repeat across, turn.

Rows 34 (36, 38) to 57 (59, 61): Work even on armhole side and decrease one patt rep on center front every other row, 5 times, then work even through last row.

Assembly

Sew shoulder seams and side seams. Weave in ends.

The sample project was made using four skeins (each 182 yards [166 m]) of 3.5-ounce (100 g) Klaus Koch Kollection's Clip 100% Egyptian cotton yarn in color #188.

YOU WILL NEED

4 (4, 5) skeins, each 3.5 oz (100 g) sport-weight pima cotton yarn

Size F crochet hook

Scissors

Tapestry needle

Abbreviations

See page 140

Stitches Used

ch

dc

sl st

Gauge

6 pattern repeats = 4 inches (10.2 cm)

8 rows = 4 inches (10.2 cm)

CLASSIC GRANNY SQUARE AFGHAN

Chances are you have a granny square afghan in your home somewhere, stored in a box in your attic or thrown over the sofa in your rec room. While the design is classic, you might find the colors a little too retro for your new millennial decor. This updated version of the beloved afghan pairs the charms of the original with a modern color palette.

YOU WILL NEED

Approximately 2 skeins of 3.5 oz (100 g) worsted-weight yarn in the following colors: tan, warm brown, copper, bronze, and berry (you may need more or less of some colors, depending on the colors you choose for your squares)

4 skeins of 3.5 oz (100 g) worsted-weight yarn in coffee

Size H crochet hook

Scissors

Large tapestry needle

Abbreviations

See page 140

Gauge

One finished square = 4 3/4 inches (12 cm)

Stitches Used

ch

dc

sl st

sc

Skill Level

Intermediate

Finished Size

Approximately 42 x 48 inches (1 x 1.2 m)

Single Granny Square (make 56 in a variety of colors, half ending in dark colors and half ending in light colors)

Foundation: Ch 4, turn.

Row 1: [2 dc, (ch 2, 3 dc) three times] into the 4th ch from hk, ch 2, sl st in the top of ch-4, do not turn, cut your yarn and weave in end.

Row 2: Attach a different color of yarn to one of the ch-2 spaces with a slip knot, ch 3, (2 dc, ch 2, 3 dc) in the same ch sp, [ch 1, (3 dc, ch 2, 3 dc) in the next ch sp] 3 times, ch 1, sl st in the top of the ch-3, cut your yarn and weave in end.

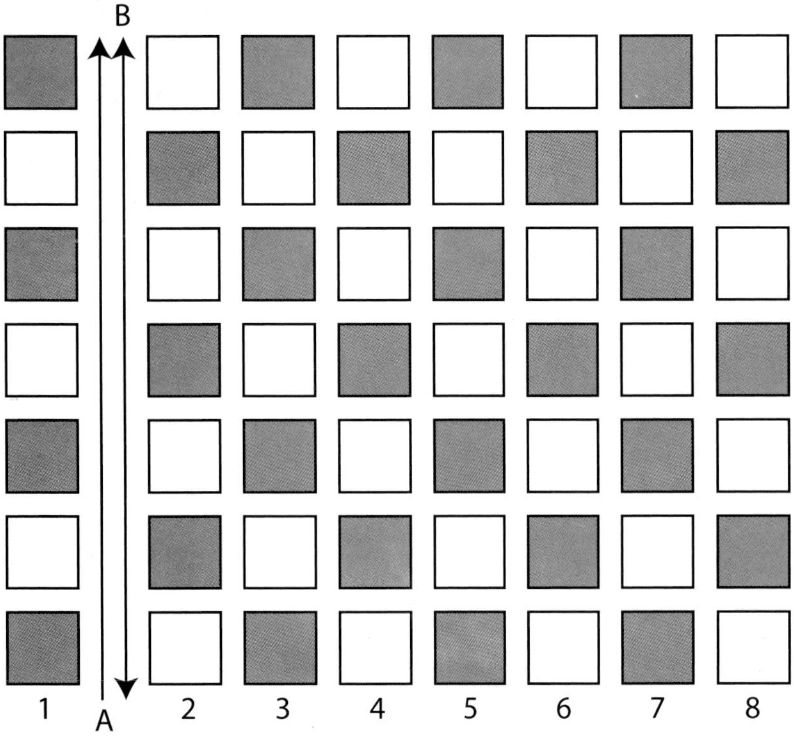

Row 3: Attach a different color of yarn to one of the ch-2 spaces with a slip knot, ch 3, (2 dc, ch 2, 3 dc) in the same ch sp, [ch 1, 3 dc in the next ch sp, ch 1, (3 dc, ch 2, 3 dc) in the next ch sp] 3 times, ch 1, 3 dc in the next ch sp, ch 1, sl st in the top of the ch-3, cut yarn and weave in end.

Row 4: Attach a different color of yarn to one of the ch-2 spaces with a slip knot, ch 3, (2 dc, ch 2, 3 dc) in the same ch sp, [(ch 1, 3 dc in the next ch sp) twice, ch 1, (3 dc, ch 2, 3 dc) in the next ch sp] 3 times, (ch 1, 3 dc in the next ch sp) twice, ch 1, sl st in the top of the ch-3, cut your yarn and weave in end.

Assembly

Lay the squares out in a light-dark checkerboard pattern (figure 1).

Work one row of squares at a time. Beginning with the first square in the first row (A in figure 1), attach the coffee-colored yarn to one of the ch-2 corners of the square, [(ch 5, sl st in the next ch sp along the edge of the square) four times, ch 5, sl st in the ch-2 corner of the next granny square] repeat for all the squares in the row, (ch 5, sl st in the next ch sp along the edge of the square) four times, ch 4.

Now work in the next row (B in figure 1), starting with the square next to the last one you added from the first row, pick up the square in the second row, sl st in the ch-2 corner of the square [(ch 2, sl st around the last ch-5 you made in the last square of the first row], ch 2, sl st in the next ch sp on the current square you are adding.

Repeat this pattern of (ch 2, sl st in the next ch-5 of the first row square, then ch 2, sl st in the next ch sp on the square you are adding) until you have attached all of the second row to the first row. Ch 4, sl st in the ch-2 sp at the corner of the very first square you began with. You will have two rows of squares attached along one side, with a zigzag diamond pattern holding them together. Cut your yarn and weave in the ends.

Figure 1

Repeat the process for each row, starting with the other side of row 2, working along the loose sides with the (ch-5, sl st) pattern, then work back the other way, adding the squares in row 3 one at a time with the (ch-2, sl st in the ch-5, ch 2, sl st in the ch sp on the new square) pattern. Once you have added all the squares together, work the same pattern, attaching all the squares together in the crosswise direction so all the squares are connected.

Border

Row 1: Attach the coffee-colored yarn to one of the ch-2 corners of a corner square. Ch 3, (2 dc, ch 2, 3 dc) in the same ch sp, (ch 1, 3 dc in the next ch sp) 4 times, [ch 1, dc in the ch-4 connecting the two squares together, (ch 1, 3 dc in the next ch sp) 5 times] repeat across one side of the afghan, ch 2, 3 dc in the same ch sp, work the same pattern around the afghan, ending with sl st in the starting ch 3.

Row 2: Ch 1, sc in ea st and ch sp around the afghan working the corners with (sc, ch-2 sc) in the corner ch-2 sp. End with a sl st in the ch-1. Cut your yarn and weave in the end.

Row 3: Repeat row 2 with the bronze yarn. Cut your yarn and weave in end.

Row 4: Attach the rust yarn to one of the ch-2 corners. Ch 3, 5 dc in the same ch sp, dc in ea st across to the next corner, 6 dc in the corner ch-2 sp, repeat the pattern around, ending with a sl st in the top of the ch-3. Cut your yarn and weave in end.

The sample project was made using one skein of Coats and Clark's 3.5 ounce (100 g) worsted-weight 100% acrylic yarn in Red Heart Classic; one skein in Copper #289; two skeins each in Tan #0334, Warm Brown #0336, Bronze #0286, and New Berry #0760; and four skeins in Coffee #0365.

HIPPIE HAPPENINGS

From sit-ins to teach-ins, be-ins to love ins, all kinds of hippie "happenings" brought like-minded people together in the '60s. A happening, the invention of the Beats in the '50s, was a one-of-a-kind event involving visual art, theatrical performance, music, light shows, and any other kind of creative expression that participants could come up with. By the '60s, happenings had turned political and often involved protesting the Vietnam War. But others were just events to celebrate love and enjoy the company of several thousand other young, beautiful people with flowers in their hair and body paint all over themselves.

The "First Ever Human Be-In" was held in San Francisco's Golden Gate Park in January of 1967. It was billed as "The Gathering of the Tribes"—an event that would bring together 20,000 people to promote harmony and understanding. Jefferson Airplane and the Grateful Dead played music, and participants banged drums, danced, and listened to speakers, including Gary Snyder and Jerry Rubin. Allen Ginsberg read poetry and led the crowd in chants. It was during this event that Timothy Leary is said to have coined his most famous phrase, "Tune in, turn on, drop out."

Later that year, a group of Haight Ashbury counterculture leaders got together and proclaimed the summer of 1967 as the "Summer of Love." Although it was to be a national celebration of life, love, and expanded consciousness, anybody who was really a hippie was in San Francisco that sum-

Claude Allen, a University of Cincinnati English professor, paints the word "love" with flourescent paint on a woman's back at a love-in at Eden Park, Ohio on April 23, 1967.
© AP/WIDE WORLD PHOTO

University of Georgia, 1969

mer. The population of Haight Ashbury reportedly swelled to 100,000 with the influx of kids determined to be where it was at. One of the biggest events of the summer was the Monterey Pop Festival, held in June. Jimi Hendrix, The Who, The Mamas and the Papas, and Ravi Shankar were among the many bands who played for the crowd of 70,000 over the three days of the event.

The landmark event of the hippie era was, of course, Woodstock, the music festival in 1969 in Bethel, New York. Planners had expected up to 100,000 for the four-day festival. In reality, about 400,000 showed up to hear Jimi Hendrix, Janis Jopin, Santana, and many, many others play. Woodstock came to symbolize everything that was right about the hippie movement. Despite a lack of food, water, shelter, and sanitation, heavy downpours, and mud every-

Sit-in, Chicago, IL, 1969

where, the crowd shared everything and remained

THE POPULATION OF HAIGHT ASHBURY SWELLED TO 100,000

peaceful. It was proof that the hippie ideal of harmony and community really could work. Later that year, however, there was a less successful result at a Rolling Stones concert in Altamont, California. The Hell's Angels, who had had a strange alliance with the hippie movement for years, were providing security for the concert. A man near the stage began waving a gun and ended up dead.

Not all the major hippie events revolved around music. The Democratic Convention of 1968 became a symbol of how volatile the antiwar movement had become. The city of Chicago had called in the National Guard and employed almost every officer on the squad to "keep the peace" during the convention. What they actually did was incite more violence, initiating attacks on protesters who chanted "The whole world is watching!" (It was one of the first times such a protest had been televised live.) The Chicago Eight, antiwar leaders including Jerry Rubin, Tom Hayden, and Abbie Hoffman, went on trial for inciting the riots. They were later acquitted.

Peace vigil, 1969

Macramé

For a long time, macramé was something of an obscure craft. It originated in Turkey as far back as the sixteenth century, was revived by nineteenth-century sailors, then disappeared again for nearly a century. Suddenly, in the '60s, macramé was back and everyone was doing it. Macramé accessories, such as belts and purses, were the latest trend, and you could hardly enter a home or restaurant without finding a macramé plant hanger in front of a window. Macramé is easy to learn and portable, and the materials are inexpensive, so it was the perfect craft for free-spirited folks with lots of creativity but not a lot of money. Like many fads, macramé fell from favor, so strongly associated with the '60s and '70s that it seemed instantly dated. But new materials, colors, and designs have brought macramé back, better than ever. Try these simple, stylish projects that breathe new life into an old favorite. If you need some reminders on macramé knots and techniques, see the reference section on pages 142-143.

Photos left to right: Sky relaxing in a macramé hammock; students from the Fashion Institute of Technology wearing macramé designs © BETTMAN/CORBIS; *The macramé park in Bolinas, California; Dress by Linda Allen.*

Designer: Jim Gentry

Marrakech Express Belt

a little bit funky and very stylish, this belt is very quick to make. For a different look, try creating the same patterns with silk cord.

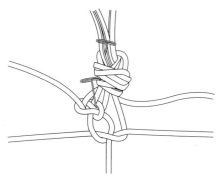

Figure 1

Figure 2

Figure 3

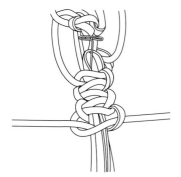

Figure 4

Figure 5

1 Hold the five suede cords together, identify their midpoint, and tie an overhand knot using all five strands.

2 Use a T-pin to anchor the overhand knot to the foam board. Arrange the cords with the two maroons on the outside and the three browns in the middle. Pick up the maroon cord on the left, combine it with two brown cords to the right, and tie one square knot using one knot-bearing cord. Lay the maroon cord to the side. Tie one square knot with the three brown cords. Pull the knot up to and just below the first knot you tied (figure 1).

3 Pick up the maroon cord on the right, combine it with two brown cords, and tie one square knot. Tie one square knot with the three brown cords. Pull the knot up to and just below the first knot you tied (figure 2).

4 Repeat steps 2 and 3 six times. You've completed almost half the belt (figure 3).

5 Use the maroon cords as knotting strands. Tie three square knots around the brown cords. Pull the last knot snugly (figure 4). Remove the T-pin from the overhand knot and untie the knot. Anchor the belt to the board. Knot the second half of the belt as described in steps 2, 3, and 4. Repeat the design sequence of four knots a total of nine times.

6 Finish the ends of the leather cords with coil knots (figure 5). Vary the position of the coil knots if you wish to create different lengths for the cord ends.

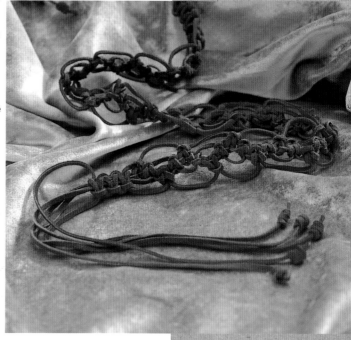

All You Need Is Love Beads Necklace

Designer: Joan Morris

The pretty wooden beads woven into this necklace are the next generation of love beads. Hemp is easy to manipulate and holds knots well, so you'll find this a quick project to complete. Lengthen or shorten the necklace by adding knots or leaving knots out.

You Will Need

1 cord hemp string, 3 yards (2.7 m) long

Necklace closure (barrel clasp)

1 cord hemp string, 1½ yards (1.3 m) long

Foam board

T-pins (to hold the necklace in place while you work)

Thread that matches hemp

Wooden beads, 4 round; 1 oval (beads' holes must accommodate 2 cords)

Sewing needle

1. Run the 3-yard (2.7 m) cord through one end of the necklace closure and to the center of the cord.

2. Find the center of the 1½-yard (1.3 m) cord and line it up with the 3-yard (2.7 m) cord at the closure. Tie an overhand knot (see page 143) to hold both cords together.

3. Secure your work to the foam board with the T-pins, positioning it so the shorter cords are in the center between the longer cords. Then tie three square knots (see page 143).

4. Drop ½ inch (1.3 cm) and tie one square knot. Repeat this five more times, dropping ½ inch (1.3 cm) between each knot.

5. String your first round bead onto the two center cords, and tie a square knot to hold it in place.

6. Drop ½ inch (1.3 cm) and tie one square knot, then drop another ½ inch (1.3 cm) and tie another square knot.

7. String the second round bead onto the two center cords, and tie a square knot to hold it in place.

8. Drop ½ inch (1.3 cm) and tie one square knot, then drop another ½ inch (1.3 cm) and tie another square knot.

9. String the oval bead over the two center cords, and tie a square knot to hold it in place. Repeat this pattern to string the remaining two round beads.

10. Repeat the square knots at ½-inch (1.3 cm) drops five times, and at the end make three square knots.

11. Turn the last square knots under and stitch in place, then stitch the other end of the necklace closure.

YESTERDAY'S MACRAME
Collar by Jack Dunstan
PHOTO COURTESY OF JEAN RAY LAURY AND JOYCE AIKEN

Designer: Jim Gentry

Taos Cowboy Hatband

The beauty of the mountains and desert attracted a lot of free spirits to the Southwest in the '60s. The combination of hippie spirit with Southwestern traditions produced an eclectic look that's echoed in this stylish hatband.

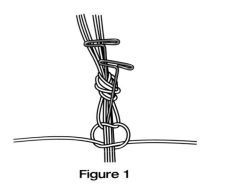

Figure 1

1 With all six cords together, tie an overhand knot at the midpoint. Anchor the cords to the foam board with a T-pin through the overhand knot.

2 Use the two outermost cords to tie one square knot around the four remaining cords (figure 1).

3 With the two outside cords inactive, use the four remaining cords to tie two square knots (figure 2).

4 String one black glass bead on each of the inactive outside cords. Use these cords to tie one square knot over the four remaining cords. The glass beads are held in place by the knot (figure 3).

5 Anchor the outside cord on the right with a T-pin below the square knot made in the previous step. Hold the cord diagonally across the remaining five cords. Tie one row of diagonal double half hitches (figure 4).

6 Tie one square knot using the four cords on the right side. Next, tie one square knot using the four cords on the left side. Then tie one square knot using the four cords on the right side.

7 Anchor the outside cord on the left side with a T-pin. Hold the cord diagonally across and down over the remaining five cords. Tie a row of diagonal double half hitches (figure 5). This completes your first pattern. Repeat steps 2 through 7 four times.

8 Remove the overhand knot, and anchor the knotting with a T-pin. To make the design units symmetrical, you need to anchor the outside cord on the left for the first row of diagonal double half hitches, working left to right. Also, you will tie the first square knot using the four strands on the left.

9 Wrap the knotting around the crown of the hat to estimate the needed length. Then join the two ends with a square knot. Trim the ends about 1 inch (2.5 cm) from the knot. If desired, secure the knot with a dab of clear-drying white craft glue.

Figure 2

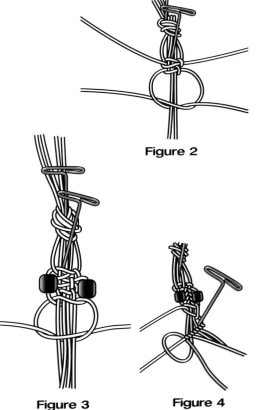

Figure 3

Figure 4

Figure 5

You Will Need

6 cords fine of hemp twine, each cut 64 inches (1.6 m) long

Foam board

T-pins

20 black glass beads, approximately 3/8 inch (9.5 mm) in diameter

Scissors

Clear-drying white craft glue (optional)

If You're Going to San Francisco

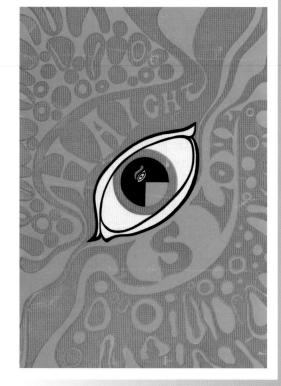

Although the hippie phenomenon was a global one to a certain extent, some cities and towns were groovier than others. Dubuque, Iowa, for example, was not a hotbed of hippie activity. In fact, hippies were seen as something of an oddity in most towns in America's heartland. San Francisco, on the other hand,

Jerry Garcia & Phil Lesh.
© TED STRESHINSKY/CORBIS

was the universally recognized epicenter of hippie culture.

The Beat writers and poets who had spawned the hippie movement started out in Greenwich Village in New York, an area long known as a haven for artists and other bohemians. But in the late '50s, many of the prominent Beats, such as Allen Ginsberg and Jack Kerouac, started hanging out in the North Beach area of San Francisco. They joined forces with Lawrence Ferlinghetti, Gary Snyder, and other writers living in the area, and soon it was the hub of everything beatnik.

Meanwhile, as the United States escalated its involvement in Vietnam, students at the nearby University of California at Berkley demanded the right to protest on campus, took over administration buildings, and started the Free Speech Movement. Berkley became known as the capital of the antiwar movement, too.

The potent combination of artists and activists made the San Francisco area a magnet for those seeking an artistic or political atmosphere. Young people started coming to town in droves, and most of them settled in a neighborhood called Haight Ashbury. "Hashbury," as it came to be known, was an area of run-down Victorian mansions rented out to students and blue-collar workers. As word got around about Haight Ashbury, run-aways, hippies, and hippie wannabes flocked to the area, find-ing cheap "crash pads" where they could stay (sometimes 20 or more to an apartment) for a few weeks, months, or years, to soak up the vibe. During the "Summer of Love" in 1967, the population of Haight Ashbury purportedly swelled to 25,000 people within a 17-block area. "Psychedelic shops" that sold books, posters, rolling papers, pipes, and love beads served the population's needs. The ballrooms of grand old Victorian homes were converted in music venues (most famously the Filmore and Avalon) where concerts and festivals featured the best local bands, including the Grateful Dead, Big Brother and the Holding Company (featuring Janis Joplin), Jefferson Airplane, and Country Joe and the Fish. Dozens of underground newspapers were published in the area. A free clinic opened in Haight Ashbury to serve the many runaways and help them recover from addiction. The Diggers, a political/theatre group provided free food for those in need at the local park. Whatever

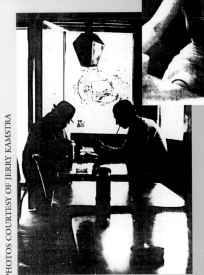

PHOTOS COURTESY OF JERRY KAMSTRA

The Beat scene in San Francisco and New York preceded the hippie era and was a direct cultural influence.

runaways, hippies, and hippie wannabes flocked to Haight Ashbury

was cutting edge and experimental politically or culturally, it was happening in Haight Ashbury.

Outside of San Francisco, there were vibrant hippie scenes in Los Angeles (Venice Beach and the Sunset Strip), New York (St. Mark's Place and the East Village), and in certain towns in the Southwest, such as Taos, Santa Fe, and Sedona. Hippie ideals flourished in communes located in rural areas all over the country, and on col-lege campuses and other areas were students gathered. Even as far away as Goa, India, and Kathmandu, Nepal, a wandering flower child could find kindred spirits and perhaps a good smoke in a hippie tea house.

Hippie travelers en route to India, 1972

Designer: Joan Morris

Blue Heaven Plant Hanger

bringing a little of Mother Nature's creations indoors was a big priority in hippie homes. This plant hanger, an updated version of the ones spotted everywhere in the '60s and '70s, gives the classic design new life with a splash of color.

1. Paint the wooden beads (and the pot, if desired) with the craft paint. Once the beads dry, spray them (and the pot, if painted) with a coat of the polyurethane. Let the polyurethane dry while you begin to macramé.

2. Hold the eight 9-yard (8.2 m) cords tightly together as a group and fold them in half to find their center. Fold the 2-yard (1.8 m) cord in half and use a lark's head knot (see page 143) to attach it to the bundle of eight cords at a point 2 inches (5.2 cm) down from its center (figure 1).

3. Use the strands of the 2-yard (1.8 m) cord to tie square knots over the bundle of cords for 4 inches (10.2 cm) (figure 2).

4. Fold the knotted bundle of cords in half, and then wrap the entire bundle (16 cords) with about 3 inches (7.6 cm) of square knots (figure 3).

5. At this point, you'll probably want to hang the piece from a hook or nail to make it easier to work with.

6. At the bottom of the 3 inches (7.6 cm) bound with square knots, divide the cords into four groups of four cords each. Tie the ends of the 2-yard (1.8 cm) cord in a regular knot in the center of the four groups of four cords. Trim the ends if necessary and secure the knot with a drop or two of the glue.

7. Tie each of the four groups of cords into chains of 12 square knots each.

8. Run a 1-inch (2.5 cm) bead up the center two cords of each of the four groups, and tie a half knot to hold the bead in place. From here, tie 5 inches (12.7 cm) of a half knot sinnet (figure 4) on each piece.

9. At the bottom of the 5 inches (12.7 cm), add another 1-inch (2.5 cm) bead onto the center two cords of each group. Follow this with a chain of 10 square knots.

10. At the bottom of each of the four chains, tie a Josephine knot (figure 5).

11. Take two cords from each adjacent Josephine knot, measure down 5 inches (12.7 cm), and tie another Josephine knot. This starts to create the basket that will hold the pot.

12. Now take two cords from each of these adjacent Josephine knots, measure down 3 inches (7.6 cm), and tie four more Josephine knots (figure 6).

13. Place the pot in the holder and gather all the cords tightly in a bunch at the center of the bottom of the pot. Use two of the cords to tie large square knots around the remaining cords for 1 inch (2.5 cm).

14. Place the 2-inch (5.2 cm) bead through all but two of the cords. Use these two cords to tie square knots around the remaining cords for 1 inch (2.5 cm).

15. Measure down about 12 inches (30.5 cm) and cut the cords evenly. You can leave them as they are or ravel their ends slightly.

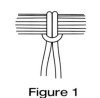

Figure 1

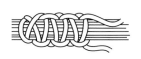

Figure 2

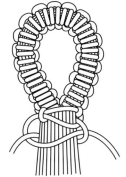

Figure 3

Figure 4

Figure 5

Figure 6

Natural Woman Belt

Designer: Joan Morris

The earthy texture of this jute cord will make you feel like a natural woman. It's easy to make in a few hours once you learn the knots. This belt looks great with clothes in other natural fibers, such as linen and cotton.

1 Fold the jute cords in half and attach each one to both buckles at once with a lark's head knot (figure 1). This will give you 16 pieces hanging from the buckles. You may find it easier to work on this project if you hang it from a hook or a doorknob.

2 Starting at the left side, take four cords and tie a square knot. Continue across until you have four square knots under the buckle. Now tie three square knots across using two cords from each of the above knots.

3 Next, tie four square knots across again like the original row. This creates the alternating knots.

4 Tie two more square knots under the four to create four short chains of square knots.

5 Now alternate on two more rows of square knots.

6 Using figure 2 as a guide, tie a row of horizontal double half hitches, across and back.

7 Below this, tie a row of diagonal double half hitches (figure 3).

8 Tie another row of horizontal double half hitches, across and back.

9 Now do three rows of the alternating square knots.

10 Divide the cords in two (eight on each side). Tie two large square knot chains, doubling up the cords. Tie eight square knots (figure 4).

11 Cross the two large square-knot chains, and then tie two rows of alternating square knots. To get the crossed chains to lay flat, hand-stitch them in place.

12 Now repeat the row of horizontal double half hitches, the row of diagonal double half hitches, and the row of horizontal double half hitches.

13 Tie four rows of alternating square knots.

14 Tie four rows of half-knot sennits, each about 1 inch (2.5 cm) long (figure 5).

15 The rows of half-knot sennits are the center of the symmetrical part of the belt's pattern. Now you'll work your way back-ward, repeating the pattern until you finish the last row of alternating square knots.

16 After the alternating square knots, tie three rows of horizontal half hitches, divide the cords in two and tie two large chains of three square knots.

17 Bring together all the cords into one large square knot. Tie a large chain of four square knots. Tie more if you need the belt to be longer. Separate the cords into four groups of four and tie overhand knots at different lengths, two knots on two of the cords, and one knot on the other two cords.

18 At the end of each cord, tie a coil knot (figure 6).

Figure 1

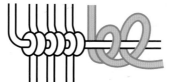

Figure 2

 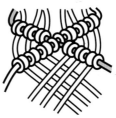

Figure 4

Figure 3

Figure 5

Figure 6

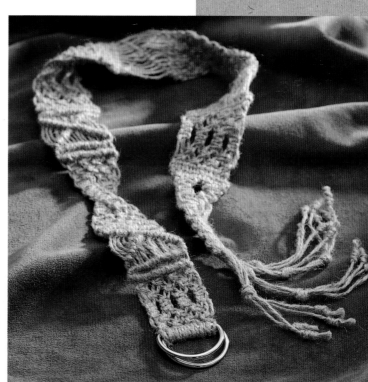

You Will Need

8 cords of natural 2-ply jute, each cut 9 yards (8.2m) long

2 half-round metal belt buckles

Sewing needle

Thread that matches jute

Scissors

Designer: Joan Morris

Haight Street Market Bag

hippie girls were often seen carrying bags just like this one to the local health food store for a few provisions. You can use it for the same purpose today, or carry it as a beach tote.

Illustrations on page 78

1 Fold the cords in half to find their centers, and mount them to the handles with a reverse lark's head knot as shown in figures 1 through 4 (attach 12 cords to each handle). You may find it easier to work on this project if you hang the wooden handles from a hook or a doorknob.

2 Divide the cords into groups of four and make six chains of square knots (figures 5 through 8) on each handle. Tie eight knots in each chain (figures 9 through 12).

3 When you've finished making all 12 chains of square knots, take one handle and begin the bag's net pattern as follows: Ignoring the two outermost cords on either end, take two cords from each adjacent group, measure down 1 inch (2.5 cm) and tie one square knot. Continue this to the end of the row.

4 Drop down 1 inch (2.5 cm) and tie the second row of square knots in staggered formation, this time including the two outermost cords on either end. Once you've finished this second row of knots, repeat this same process (steps 3 and 4) with the second handle.

5 Now join the two handle sides together by dropping down 1 inch (2.5 cm) and tying the two adjacent end cords from each handle together in a square knot. Continue with this staggered third row of knots until you join the other side (figure 13).

6 Continue staggering rows of square knots until you have completed 12 rows.

7 Finish the bottom of the bag by knotting together one cord from the front and one cord from the back all the way along the bottom. You can either pull the leftover cords to the inside and cut them or leave them on the outside and trim them even to create fringe.

You Will Need

24 cords of 5-ply jute, each cut 3½ yards (3.2 m) long*

2 circular wooden handles, each 6 inches (15.2 cm) in diameter

Measuring tape

Scissors

*If you use a thinner jute, you'll need to increase the amount of jute and the number of rows you start with.

YESTERDAY'S MACRAMÉ
Macramé by Jack Dunstan
PHOTO COURTESY OF JEAN RAY LAURY
& JOYCE AIKEN

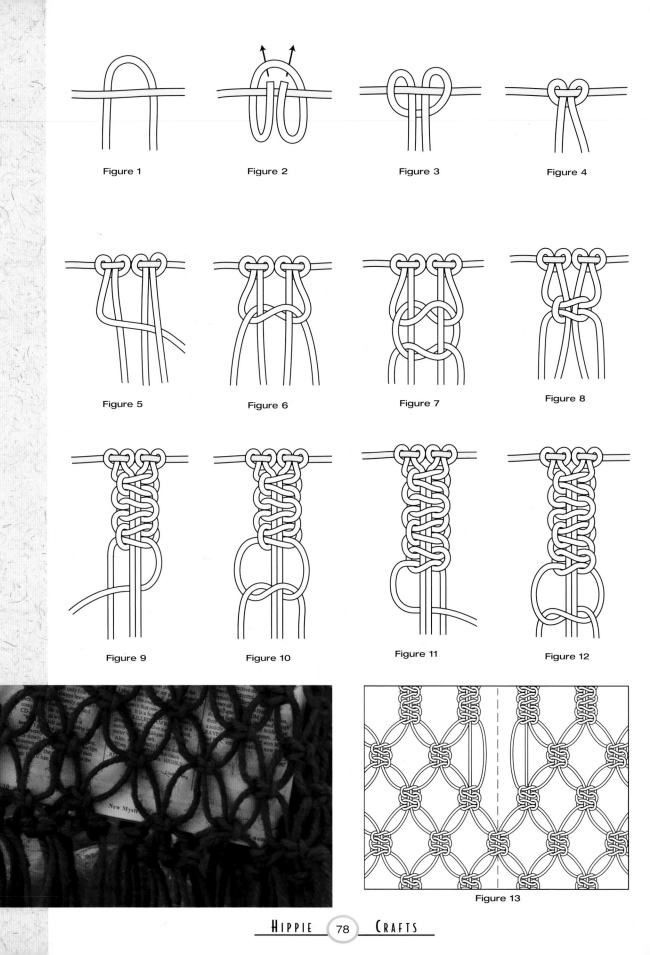

Figure 1

Figure 2

Figure 3

Figure 4

Figure 5

Figure 6

Figure 7

Figure 8

Figure 9

Figure 10

Figure 11

Figure 12

Figure 13

California Dreamin' Pillow

Designer: Jim Gentry

ay your head on this groovy pillow for mellow dreams. It's a laid-back look that's easy to create with basic macramé skills.

You Will Need

44 pieces of nylon crochet cord, each cut 36 inches (.9 m) long

T-pins

Foam board marked with a 12 x 12-inch (30.5 x 30.5 cm) grid of 1 inch (2.5 cm) squares*

12-inch (30.5 cm) square pillow

Scissors

Ruler or tape measure

Straight pins

Sewing needle

Thread

*If you don't wish to mark a grid on your foam board, mark the grid on a piece of paper the same size as your board. Pin or tape the paper to the board.

1 Separate the cords into 11 groups of four cords each. Tie an overhand knot at the midpoint of each group of four cords. Anchor the overhand knots with T-pins equally spaced on the centerline of the marked foam board.

2 Tie two square knots in each group of four cords. Anchor each group of finished knots with a T-pin to the line on the grid. Starting at the point where you regroup your cords into groups of four (with two cords inactive on the left and right) tie two square knots in each of the new groups of four (figure 1). There will be 10 groups of square knots in the second row when completed.

3 Tie an overhand knot in each of the two unknotted, inactive strands on the left and right sides. Center each overhand knot on the grid line and secure it with a T-pin.

4 Work four more alternating rows made up of square knots and overhand knots for a total of six rows in all (figure 2). Work a seventh row of square knots, this time with three square knots in each group of four. Tie an overhand

knot in each group, pulling snugly against the last square knot (figure 3).

5 Turn the board upside down. Remove the T-pins from the first row of pinned overhand knots. Move the pins to the first row of square knots. Untie the overhand knots. Follow the knotting directions in steps 2 through 4. Finish this end with overhand knots.

6 If the pillow has a removable cover, remove the pillow. Otherwise, center the overlay on the pillow. Pin it to the pillow on all sides with the straight pins.

7 Thread a needle with thread to match the pillow cover. Hand-stitch the knotted piece to the pillow, catching each knotted end around the outer edge of the pillow. The knots may be stitched to the cover in the center of the pillow, if desired.

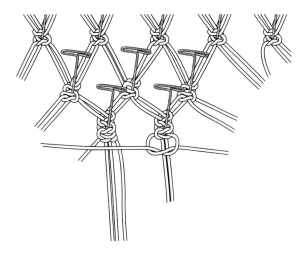

Figure 1

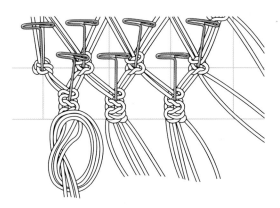

Figure 2

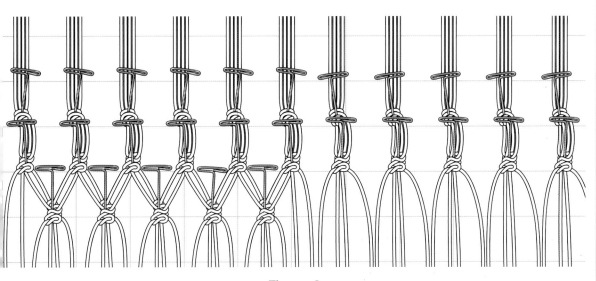

Figure 3

Everybody Get Together...
Hippie Communes

What were hippie communes? The mainstream media portrayed them as hotbeds of free love and radical ideas. They showed images of dirty hippies lying around smoking pot in broken-down rural houses. The alternative media showed them as utopian paradises where workers controlled the means of production and lived outside the consumer-driven culture. Both portrayals con-

tained a grain of truth. Although communes started out as a way for people to work together for the common good, share resources, and live a life true to their beliefs, many ended up as noble, but failed, experiments.

Drop City near Trinidad, Colorado, was the forerunner of communes to come. The members lived in geodesic domes made out of recycled car parts and sold scrap metal for money. In communes such as the Hog Farm and New Buffalo in New Mexico, members lived in tepees and grew their own food. The Farm, just outside Nashville, Tennessee, was perhaps the most famous. Started by hippie philosopher Stephen Gaskin, the Farm was settled by a group that started out from San Francisco in a 20-bus caravan in 1971 with the slogan "Out to Save the World." The members not only operated a farm, but they also started a publishing company that published one of the first vegetarian cookbooks and started a midwifery school credited with reviving the practice in the United States.

But as commune members started putting theories and ideals to the test, a number of issues surfaced. Although many loved the idea of working the land and building everything themselves, not everyone had the skills to make the dream a reality. Poor workmanship led to drafty houses, leaky roofs, and crumbling walls, which in turn led to dissatisfaction. Even though gender equality was supposed to be part of the new way of life, many commune women complained that they ended up doing most of the work while the men played music and smoked pot. Living with others and sharing the workload had its perks, but many found that they missed the privacy and freedom of living on their own. And finally, even though the point of communes was to live outside capitalist society, it was difficult to do so in reality. The need for money was always there and always a source of struggle and tension.

Group portrait of family of the Mystic Arts Commune in front of their home, Jan. 1, 1969.
© JOHN OLSON/TIME LIFE PICTURE/GETTY IMAGES

Disenchanted with the idea of communal living, many members integrated themselves back into the mainstream by the end of the '70s. Other communes adapted and survived, changing their more stringent rules to allow members to own their own property while keeping a stake in the community property. Many developed successful income-gener- ating businesses that allowed members to make a living

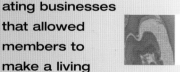

not everyone had the skills to make the dream a reality

and keep their ideals intact. During the '80s and '90s, a less rigid form of commune, called an intentional community, developed. These communities, just as often in urban or even suburban areas as in the country, feature indi- vidual-owned family homes grouped close together around communally owned property. The members share chores and meals but work outside the community and create their own income, striking a balance between ideals and reality.

PHOTO COURTESY OF JEAN RAY LAURY AND JOYCE AIKEN

beather

Although it might surprise some modern-day hippies (especially vegans), leather was a favorite with hippie crafters. Many saw it as a return to nature after the space-age craze and Mod clothing. For some it had a nostalgic appeal, harkening back to the frontier of the old West, when self-reliant pioneers made all their own clothing using animal skins they purchased from local tribes. It was the revival of a time-honored tradition, done by skilled craftspeople, not churned out on machines. Whatever the reason, leather fringed vests were a must for men, and women who had the skill made their own fringed purses. Leather hair accessories complemented the long, straight hair favored by hippie girls. And of course there were the belts, again with lots of fringe hanging freely. With new fabrics, leather crafts are easier than ever to make, and new embellishments update the hippie standards with style.

Santa Fe Fringe Vest

Designer: Joan Morris

Roger Daltrey wore one onstage at Woodstock. Grace Slick had one, too. A fringed leather vest was the ultimate in cool and still is. Although '60s hippies had to use real leather, you can use a more modern alternative—synthetic suede. It's easy to work with and butter-soft to the touch.

1 With the craft paper and pencil, make a life-size pattern using the diagram below.

2 Place the suede down on the pattern with the cut ends at the top and bottom. Pin the pattern to the suede and cut it out. Save the scraps.

3 Lay the back piece of the vest on the rotary cutter mat. Use the marked measurements on the mat to cut the fringe. Start at the bottom and cut up 7 inches (17.8 cm) every 1/2 inch (1.3 cm) across the width of the piece. Use a ruler to keep the cuts straight.

4 Repeat step 3 with both front pieces.

5 Cut two pieces of scrap suede, each 5 x 9 inches (12.7 x 22.9 cm). Cut one piece of suede 11 x 14 inches (28 x 35.6 cm).

6 Find the center of one of the 5 x 9-inch (12.7 x 22.9 cm) pieces of suede. Measure down 2 inches (5.1 cm) from the center, then draw a line to each edge of the piece, creating a V shape. Cut out the shape.

7 Measure down 7 inches (18 cm) from the center of the V and 7 inches (18 cm) from the corners. Draw a line to make them meet and cut out the piece.

8 With the rotary tool, cut 6-inch fringe (15.2 cm) as in step 3.

9 Find the center of the 14-inch (35.6 cm) edge of the 11 x 14-inch (28 x 35.6 cm) piece. Measure down 3 inches (7.6 cm) from this point and draw a line to the corners. Cut out the piece.

10 Measure down 8 inches (20.3 cm) from the center of the V and 8 inches (20.3 cm) in from the corners. Draw a line to connect these points, then cut out the shape.

11 With the rotary tool, cut 7-inch (18 cm) fringe as in step 3.

12 Use the sewing machine to stitch the fringe in place on the front and back plackets.

13 With the right sides together, machine-stitch the shoulders and side seams.

14 Cut a strip of suede 1/4 x 18 inches (.6 x 45.7 cm).

15 With scissors or a hole punch, make a hole at each corner of the center front through which to lace the strip you just cut.

16 Run the lace through the holes and tie a bow.

17 To add the beaded embellishments, first thread your beading needle. Bring it up through your first turquoise chip, slip the sterling bead onto the thread, then run the thread back down through the chip and start sewing onto the vest from back to front. Keep threading and adding beads until you reach the edge of the vest, then tie the thread in a strong knot.

You Will Need

1 yard (91.4 cm) of craft paper

Pencil

1 yard (91.4 cm) of synthetic suede

Straight pins

Scissors

Rotary cutter and mat

Ruler

Measuring tape

Sewing machine

Matching thread

Turquoise chips

Small sterling beads

Beading thread

Beading needle

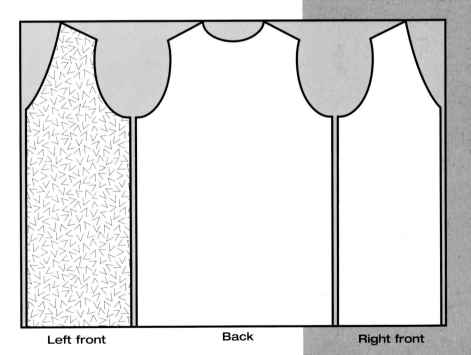

Left front   Back   Right front

flower Power Suede Headband

Designer: Joan Morris

 nce *the* radical accessory, the headband fell out of fashion as times changed. Isn't it time it made a comeback? This design updates the headband for the twenty-first century. It's soft and pretty, but it's still got plenty of flower power.

1 Choose which suede strip will be your over-lay piece, then find its center. Set a stud in this position—this is the center of a flower.

2 Using the teardrop hole punch, punch holes around the stud to make the flower petals. If you have trouble piercing the suede, try punching through the lightweight sandpaper to sharpen your hole punch.

3 Measure and place a stud about every 3 inches (7.6 cm) to create a row of flowers. Punch out the petals.

4 Use your imagination and punch rows of squares and triangles, or circles of round dots, to complete the design. Just be careful not to punch too close to the edge.

5 When you're satisfied with your design, turn over the punched piece and dot white glue all over it (avoiding the holes).

6 Place the second piece of suede on top of the piece you punched and press in place with your hand. Let dry. Cut off the corners at each end, and insert a grommet.

7 Knot one end of the 18-inch (45.7 cm) lace and run it through one of the grommets from the front and through the other grom-met from the back. Knot the other end.

You Will Need

2 pieces of synthetic suede in contrasting colors, each 2 x 24 inches (5.2 x 61 cm)

Stud setter

7 round silver studs

Teardrop hole punch

Fine sandpaper, if needed

Measuring tape

Square hole punch

Triangle hole punch

Round hole punch

White glue

Scissors

2 small grommets

Leather lace cord, 18 inches (45.7 cm) long

YESTERDAY'S LEATHER
Leather dress by Kent L. Child
PHOTO COURTESY OF JEAN RAY LAURY
AND JOYCE AIKEN

Wild Thing Ponytail Holders

At love-ins and be-ins alike, hippie girls with long tresses tied their straight hair in ponytail holders like these. They're a unique way to add a little leather to your look without going full-out fringe.

You Will Need

Scrap suede cut into 2 rectangles, about 2 x 3 inches (5.1 x 7.6 cm)

Leather punch

16 metal eyelets

Eyelet setter

Scissors

Piece of suede lace, 4-foot (1.2 m) long

1 Using the leather punch, punch out the lacing holes near the edge of the long side of each rectangle (see detail photo below).

2 Position the eyelets where you want them and set them with the eyelet setter.

3 Cut the suede lace into two 2-foot (61 cm) lengths. Thread the laces through the eyelets.

YESTERDAY'S LEATHER

Leather vest by Gordon Broft
PHOTO COURTESY OF JEAN RAY LAURY AND JOYCE AIKEN

The Psychedelic Silver Screen

By the mid-'60s, Gidget had left the building. The beach party movies that young people had flocked to in the late '50s and early '60s had already become hopelessly outdated. While film was never a big medium for expression of hippie culture, the movies of the '60s began to reflect the

We all live in a yellow submarine

same sort of break with traditional themes and forms that was seen in other media.

In 1967, *The Graduate* (United Artists) broke new ground with its insightful portrayal of the alienation of the baby-boomer youth and the widening generation gap. The adults in the movie were out of touch, shallow, and cynical, and the youth were disaffected.

Dennis Hopper and Peter Fonda in Easy Rider   © BETTMAN/CORBIS

The movie's soundtrack (CBS Records, 1967), including Simon and Garfunkel's "Mrs. Robinson," "Scarborough Fair," and "Sounds of Silence" became an instant classic. The following year, Peter Sellers starred as a thirty-some-thing square who turns hippie with the help of a free-spirited girl and some hash brownies in *I Love You, Alice B. Toklas* (Warner Brothers, 1968).

Although these films were still very mainstream and traditional in their form, other film-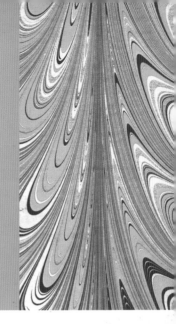makers were throwing convention to the wind. Roger Corman's *The Trip* (AIP, 1967), starring Peter Fonda and Dennis Hopper, was a simulated acid trip on film, complete with bizarre visions such as witches and dwarves, and sex under a strobe light. The movie's advertisement promised that viewers would "listen to the sound of love, feel purple, taste green," just like an acid trip. Although it's now thought to have more historical significance than artistic merit, the movie spawned a host of other psychedelic-inspired films, includ-ing; *The Love Ins* (Columbia, 1967), *Psych Out* (AIP,1968), and *Wild in the Streets* (AIP, 1968) in which a popular rock star turned politician advocates sending everyone over age 35 to LSD camps.

Even the Beatles got in on the psyche-delic trip movie scene with *Yellow Submarine* (United Artists, 1968), a far cry from their previous romps *Help!* (United Artists, 1965) and *A Hard Day's Night* (United Artists, 1964).

The movie perhaps most strongly iden-tified with hippies is *Easy Rider* (Columbia Pictures, 1969), directed by Dennis Hopper and starring Hopper and Peter Fonda. The movie follows the two protagonists as they hop on their motorcycles and ride from Los Angeles

a simulated acid trip on film, complete with bizarre visions

to New Orleans in search of "the real America." Along the way they encounter various characters, from a drunken lawyer yearning to be free (Jack Nicholson) to a commune leader to a gang of intolerant rednecks. Steppenwolf's "Born to Be Wild" blasts in the background as they motor through the desert, capturing the sense of freedom that characterized the young generation. The same year saw the debut of *Midnight Cowboy* (MGM Studios, 1969), the gritty story of two drifters whose paths cross in the streets of New York. The movie court-ed controversy with its unprecedented nudity and sex scenes. But it won best picture and best director at the Academy Awards that year, proving that audiences were ready for realism on screen.

L.A. Woman Leather Purse

Designer: Joan Morris

everyone (well, *almost* everyone) had a purse like this in the '60s. It was worn in a small size by women and in a larger satchel size by men. It's easy enough to make with the right tools, and even today it projects an image that's freewheeling and fun.

You Will Need

Scrap of leather, enough to cut into two pieces: one 8 x 20 inches (20.3 x 50.8 cm), one 8 x 24 inches (20.3 x 61 cm)

Ruler

Pen

Scissors

Rotary cutter and mat

2 grommets, each 3/8 inch (6 cm) in diameter

Leather punch

9 yards (8.2 m) of leather lace

1 Place the 8 x 20-inch (20.3 x 50.8 cm) piece of leather (this will be the front of the purse) wrong side up. Starting at one of the 8-inch (20.3 cm) sides, measure and mark every 1/4 inch (6 mm).

2 On the 20-inch (50.8 cm) side, measure up 8 inches (20.3 cm) from the bottom, and draw a line across the width of the leather. Measure and mark every 1/4 inch (6 mm) along this line.

3 If you don't have a rotary cutter, draw lines from 1/4-inch (6 mm) mark to 1/4-inch (6 mm) mark, and cut the fringe with scissors. If you do have a rotary cutter, just line up the marks with a ruler and cut with the rotary cutter.

4 Place the 8 x 24-inch (20.3 x 61 cm) piece of leather wrong side up and measure up 9 inches (22.9 cm) along the sides and 6 inches (15.2 cm) in to the center. Draw lines from the 9-inch (22.9 cm) measurement to the 6-inch (15.2 cm) measurement on both sides, making a point.

5 Mark 1/4-inch (6 mm) measurements along the bottom edge. Draw a line across the 6-inch (15.2 cm) measurement and mark every 1/4 inch (6 mm). Use scissors or a rotary cutter and cut the fringe, following the point.

6 Leave the 24-inch (61 cm) piece wrong side up and measure 12 inches (30.5 cm) up from the uncut bottom and draw a line. Place the front piece right side up on top of the back piece, with its top edge on the line and the sides matching.

7 Following the manufacturer's instructions, place the grommets at the top edge of the front piece and through the back piece. (This is where the straps will be tied.)

8 Starting just below the grommet on the edges, mark every 1/2 inch (1.3 cm) all the way around the sides and bottom.

9 Using the leather punch, punch holes through each mark.

10 Cut 3 yards (2.7 m) of leather lace. Knot one end. Starting from the front, pull the lace through the top hole on one side of the purse. Bring the lace up and run it through the second hole. Do this all the way down the first edge.

11 Weave a straight stitch across the bottom from side to side. Now start wrapping up the last side. When you reach the top, tie a knot.

12 Cut six pieces of the leather lace 1 yard (.9 m) each.

13 Take three of the cut pieces, put one end of each through one of the grommets, and tie a knot.

14 Do a simple braid all the way to the end of the pieces.

15 Repeat steps 13 and 14 on the other side.

16 Tie the ends in a large knot to finish the strap.

YESTERDAY'S LEATHER

Leather bags by Sherwin Strull
PHOTO COURTESY OF JEAN RAY LAURY AND JOYCE AIKEN

Leather Hair Thong

Designer: Allison Smith

Flowers in your hair would be your first choice, but they're not always practical or in season. This barrette is the next best thing. It's reminiscent of those worn by many a longhaired hippie girl, but the beads add just a bit more flair.

You Will Need

Pencil

Piece of scrap leather

Scissors

Awl

Leather punch

Beading thread

Beading needle

Seed beads

Long hair stick

1 Trace the template (see page 143) onto the back of the piece of leather.

2 Cut the leather along the traced outline.

3 Use the awl to punch out the bead pattern.

4 Use the leather punch to punch out the holes for the hair stick.

5 Working from the back of the leather, sew the beads through the holes you punched in step 3. Start by threading your beading needle. String five beads onto the thread, then pull the thread through the leather, front to back. Add another five beads, then pull through the next hole. Repeat the process for the last side of the triangle. The finished pattern will be a series of triangles across the top and bottom of the leather. The triangles are composed of five beads on each side.

6 Carefully secure the beading thread with a series of strong square knots on the back of the leather. Thread the hair stick through the holds you punched in step 4.

YESTERDAY'S HAIR STYLE

*Sky with a flower in her hair,
around 1968*

If you're going to San Francisco be sure to wear a flower in your hair...

If You're Not Part of the Solution...

The decade of the '60s was nothing if not political. From the civil rights movement at the start of the decade to the antiwar movement that dominated public discourse into the '70s, people of all types organized and protested like never before.

College campuses were at the center of much of the political action during the '60s. In the early '60s, Students for a Democratic Society (SDS) organized on campuses. Borrowing tactics from the successful civil rights movements, the group held teach-ins, educating students about the Vietnam War and training them to protest effectively. From campuses, the anti-

Anti-Vietnam War demonstrators run up against military police at the Pentagon, October 21, 1967.
©AP/WIDE WORLD PHOTO

war movement spread and gradually grew to include housewives, clergy, and even Vietnam vets. The first antiwar march on Washington took place in 1965, with more than 25,000 people in attendance.

The antiwar issue became more emotionally charged as thousands of young men were being shipped out to Vietnam and shipped back home in body bags every week. Antidraft demonstrations were held; young men burned their draft cards; and as fewer and fewer were granted "conscientious objector" status, many began to flee to Canada to avoid the draft and became known as "draft dodgers." By 1969, more than 400,000 people showed up at an antiwar march on Washington.

The peaceful nature of protest gradually became more violent as tensions escalated. Student organizations began calling for student strikes and took over college administration buildings, demanding changes in academic policies, such as curriculum reform and the inclusion of ethnic studies. A radical faction broke off from the SDS and called themselves the Weathermen. They advocated using violence against the government and began bombing symbols of the establishment, such as banks. Antiwar protesters stormed the Pentagon, and Vietnam vets hurled their medals over the fence of the White House. At the 1968 Democratic National Convention in Chicago, police officers and the National Guard attacked protesters led by the Yippies (Youth International Protest), including Abbie Hoffman, Tom Hayden, Jerry Rubin, and Dave Dellinger. The Chicago Eight, as the organizers were known, were tried for inciting a riot but were acquitted. Later, antiwar protesters were attacked by construction workers in New York City, and four student protesters were killed by the National Guard at Kent State in 1970.

Students protesting the war in Vietnam, November, 1969.

While the civil rights movement had advocated nonviolence, the Black Panthers, a group that formed in the mid-'60s took just the opposite tack and armed themselves heavily. Other ethnic minorities began organizing as well. Cesar Chavez brought together the underrepresented migrant workers in California and the Southwest, and Native American groups aligned in the American Indian Movement. In 1969, a group representing all tribes reclaimed Alcatraz Island in San Francisco Bay for Native Americans and stayed there until 1971.

A radical faction broke off from the SDS and called themselves the Weathermen

The women's rights movement also began in the '60s, with a push toward equal educational and job opportunities and reproductive rights. A clash between gay residents of Greenwich Village and the police in 1969 became known as the Stonewall Riots, and the gay rights movement was born.

Meanwhile, the antinuclear movement, born in the '50s, grew in momentum and "Ban the Bomb" demonstrations attracted tens of thousands of participants. And the budding ecology movement, later known as the environmental movement, got underway.

All this within the span of a decade that changed history.

Students demonstrating against the draft outside the Commerce Building in Worchester, MA, 1969.
PHOTO COURTESY OF SHARON FAHRER

Photos, left to right: Jewelry vendor at Berkley's Telegraph Avenue crafts market; Necklace by Lance Bow

JEWELRY

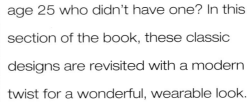

n the '60s, renewed interest in all things Native American brought beading back into style. Beaded headbands, bracelets, and medallions with Native American motifs and patterns were the perfect partners for peasant dresses or leather fringed vests. And of course, there were the peace medallions. Was there anyone under age 25 who didn't have one? In this section of the book, these classic designs are revisited with a modern twist for a wonderful, wearable look.

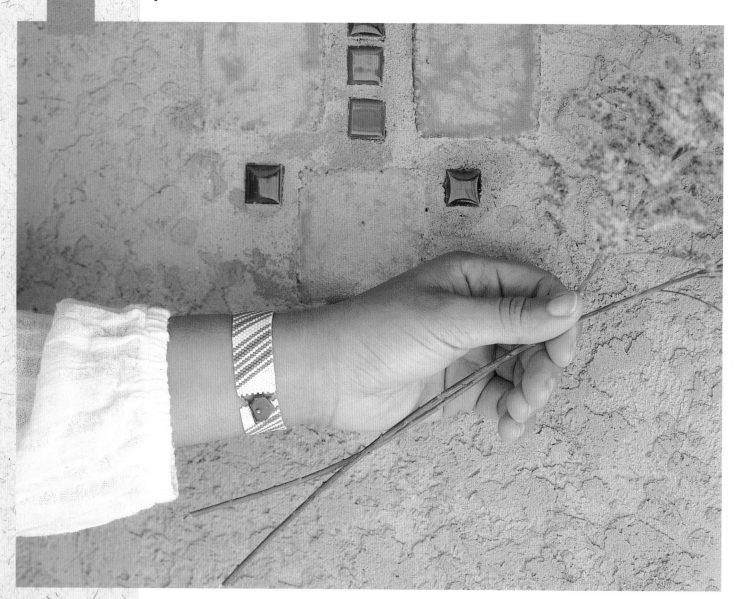

Designer: GEORGIE ANN JAGGERS

NEW BUFFALO
PEYOTE STITCH BRACELET

The turquoise and white beads in this bracelet call to mind the traditional beadwork of Native American jewelry. The flat peyote stitch is easy to create once you've got the hang of it, so you can experiment with adding more colors to your pattern if you like.

1 Cut a piece of beading thread about 4 feet (1.2 m) long. Wax or condition the thread by holding it with your thumb against the wax or conditioner and pulling. Waxing the thread not only gets the curl out, but it also protects it from moisture and fraying.

2 Thread both needles onto your waxed thread (figure 1). For best results, pinch the end of your thread between two fingers where you can just see the tip of it. Set the eye of the needle on the tip and pull the thread through, leaving about a 10-inch (25.4 cm) tail.

3 Holding one needle in each hand, put one bead (in this case, white) on one needle and two beads (also white) on the other (figure 2). It doesn't matter which needle gets one or two beads. Keep the beads on the needle—don't let them slip down to the thread yet.

4 Take the needle with one bead, and poke it through the bottom of the top bead on the other needle (figure 3).

5 Now pull all three beads down onto the thread all the way to the center to form a small pyramid (figure 4, page 104).

6 Repeat steps 3 through 5 seven times to create a stack of these pyramids, which will form the first row of the bracelet (figure 5, page 104). Vary the width of your bracelet by making fewer or more pyramids. When you've finished stacking all the pyramids, remove one of the needles and let its thread hang for now. You'll use it later to make the bracelet's clasp.

7 Make sure the needle still attached to a thread is pointing to the right, as shown in figure 6, page 104. Place a white bead on the needle and go through, in a downward motion, the bead that is jutting out to the right, one row down from the top (figure 7, page 104). Pull the thread through, add another bead, and go through the next bead down that's jutting out to the right. Continue adding beads in this manner until you get to the bottom of the row.

8 Now add a white bead to the thread and start back up into the bead that is jutting out to the right on the second row from the bottom (figure 8, page 105). Continue adding beads in this manner until you get to the top.

9 Turn around and work your way back down again (figure 9, page 105).

10 To begin the diagonal pattern, add a turquoise bead when you've reached the bottom of a row and are starting back up. Then continue with white beads—don't add another turquoise bead until you've worked your way to the top and back down. This second turquoise bead will go in the space above the first turquoise bead (figure 10, page 105). Always add the turquoise bead in the space above the last turquoise bead and a diagonal line of color will begin to form.

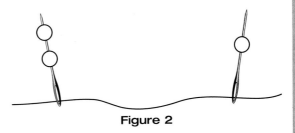
Figure 1

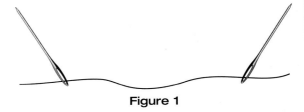
Figure 2

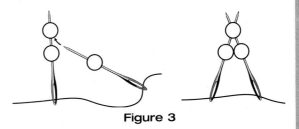
Figure 3

YOU WILL NEED

Scissors

Nylon beading thread (size D)

Beeswax or thread conditioner

Size 11 delicas, 5 grams each of 2 colors*

2 beading needles (size 12)**

Coral or stone chip (dyed red)

*A type of cylindrical bead. Use delicas (as opposed to regular seed beads) because they're more uniform in shape and their thin walls and large holes can accommodate multiple threads. Our bracelet uses white and turquoise beads. You may, of course, substitute colors of your own choosing.

**Use beading needles because they're thin and flexible and have an eye that can pass through small beads easily.

Figure 4

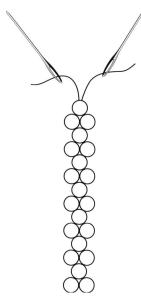

Figure 5

11 Continue working your way up and down the rows, adding in turquoise or white beads to create the color pattern shown in figure 11.

12 When about a 10-inch (25.4 cm) strand of thread is left sticking out of the top at the end of a row, it's time to change thread. Instead of adding a bead on the right, put your needle through the top bead on the left and go down in a diagonal line through three or more beads and then go up in a diagonal line through the beads on the left (figure 12). The purpose here is to bury your thread in a zigzag motion. Once this is done, put new waxed thread on your needle and tie three overlapping knots on the end. Insert the needle in the middle of the rows and zigzag back through the beads so that your needle comes out of the very top

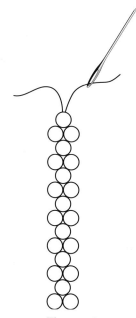

Figure 6

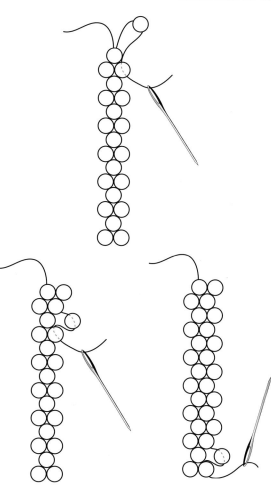

Figure 7

bead (figure 13). If you listen carefully, you'll hear your knots "pop" into the first bead you put your needle through. Now you're ready to keep on stitching.

13 Continue working the rows until your bracelet is the length desired; then it's time to add the clasp and catch. You should have two pieces of thread coming out of your bracelet, one on each end. At the end that will have the catch, run the thread back down through the beads in a zigzag motion for ¼ inch (6 mm) to a spot in the center of the bracelet's width (figure 14). Thread on two turquoise beads, the coral or stone chip, and one more turquoise bead. Run the needle back through the chip and two beads. Try to go through the beads and chip at least three times. Weave different patterns between each pass and bury your thread.

14 At the other end of the bracelet, make a loop using turquoise beads. Test the loop for size—it should fit snugly over the chip. Secure the loop by going through the bottom bead that juts out (figure 15), and then running your needle through the beads of the bracelet in an upward zigzag motion. Pass through your bead loop at least three times, weaving zigzag patterns between each pass. Bury your thread.

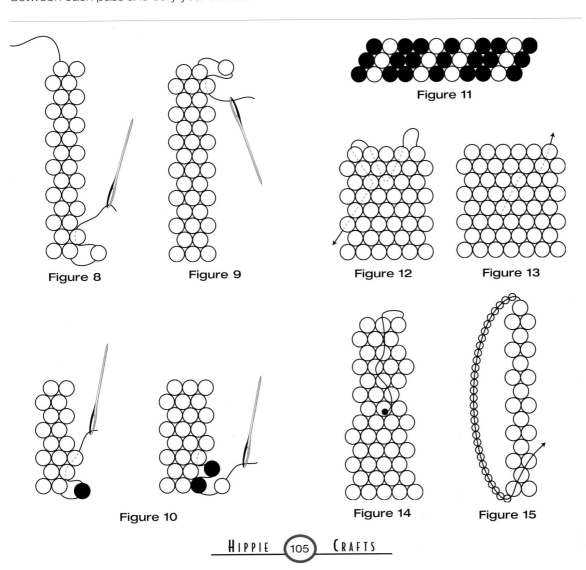

Figure 8

Figure 9

Figure 11

Figure 12

Figure 13

Figure 10

Figure 14

Figure 15

Designer: THERESE DE LA BATON ROUGE

GIVE PEACE A CHANCE MEDALLION

Peace signs were practically regulation attire for hippies. People wore them patched to their jeans, painted on their faces, or hanging around their necks. This new interpretation of the hippie icon combines easy metal jewelry skills and contemporary materials for a beautiful "peace" you'll want to show off.

1 Copy the peace sign on page 143. Adhere the template to the brass sheet with rubber cement.

2 To cut the peace sign, use the shears and a jewelry saw and cut just outside the template's lines. To get started, drill four small holes large enough to accommodate your saw blade in each of the interior sections that will be cut. Thread your saw blade though a hole, retighten your blade, and then cut out each interior section. Remove the paper template. Smooth any rough or sharp edges with the file.

3 Use the compass to create a paper circle a little larger than your brass peace sign. Adhere the circle to the copper sheet with the rubber cement. Cut out the copper circle, then smooth the edges with the file. Remove the paper template.

4 Texture the surface of the copper circle by tapping it with the ball peen hammer. Tap lightly until you discover what sort of texture your tapping creates. Increase the force for a more pronounced texture.

5 To make the holes for the copper circle's rivets, mark eight evenly spaced points around its perimeter. Select a drill bit the same size or slightly smaller than the diameter of your brass tubing, and drill a hole at each point. File any rough edges.

6 To begin making the decorative rivets, use the saw to cut the brass tubing into eight lengths slightly longer than the thickness of your copper sheet. If needed, enlarge the drilled holes to accommodate the tubing, but make sure each piece of tube fits snugly in its hole.

7 To turn the tube lengths into rivets, place each length of tubing you sawed in a hole. Place the end of an awl or a sharp nail into the tubing, and use a circular motion to flare the tubing slightly. Turn the copper piece over and flare the opposite end of the tubing. Continue to flare each rivet until it is not able to fall out of its hole.

8 Now flatten the tube rivets by tapping on each one with the ball peen hammer. Tap lightly on one side, then the other, alternating which side you work on until the rivet is flush on both sides.

9 Rub the copper disc with the scrub pad to remove any scratches and residue of glue to restore the shine.

10 The brass peace sign is riveted to the copper disc with three escutcheon pins. To begin, drill the holes for these pins in the sign—these should be the same size or slightly smaller than the diameter of your escutcheon pins. You can enlarge the holes with the needle file to fit the pin, if needed.

11 Place the brass peace sign on the copper disc, positioning it so the hole at the top of the peace sign is equidistant from two of the rivets in the copper circle. Mark and drill only one hole in the copper. Enlarge that with the file, if needed.

12 Slip an escutcheon pin through both holes. Mark where it sticks out on the back, and cut the pin slightly above the mark. (About 1 millimeter should do it.) Turn the assembly over and tap lightly (but firmly) on the cut end of the pin with the ball peen hammer until the pin begins to spread. Continue tapping until the pin holds the two pieces together snugly.

13 Drill the other two holes in the copper and then repeat step 12 with each one.

14 Use whatever cord ends you wish to attach the leather thongs to the medallion.

You Will Need

Paper and pencil

Brass sheet (24 gauge or thicker), 4 inches (10.2 cm) square*

Rubber cement

Metal shears

Jewelry saw

Drill and drill bits

Half-round file

Compass

Copper sheet (24 gauge or thicker), 4 inches (10.2 cm) square*

Ball peen hammer

12-inch (30.5 cm) length of brass tubing, 3/16 inch (5mm) in diameter *

Awl or sharp nail

Kitchen scrub pad

Brass escutcheon nails

Round needle file

Cord ends**

Leather thong or suede lacing

* The metal sheets and brass tubing can be found at most craft stores or in stores specializing in model railroading or model building.

**Available at craft and bead stores

Designer: GEORGIE ANN JAGGERS

SEDONA NECKLACE

The colors of the desert are captured in this contemporary pattern using the tubular peyote stitch technique. This pattern is for a 16 to 17-inch (40.6 to 43.2 cm) necklace.

1 Cut a piece of beading thread about 4 feet (1.2 m) long. Wax or condition your thread by holding your thumb over your thread against the wax or conditioner and pulling the thread through it. It's important to wax your thread because it not only gets the curl out, but it also protects your thread from moisture and fraying.

2 Thread the needle. For best results, pinch the end our your thread between two fingers where you can just see the tip of it. Set the eye of the needle on the tip and pull the thread through, leaving about a 10-inch (25.4 cm) tail.

3 String 22 brown delicas on the thread. Pass the needle through all the beads again, forming a loop. Insert the pencil into the loop (you'll be beading around it) (figure 1).

4 Add one bead to the thread. Skip to the next bead on the base circle and run your needle through it in the same direction that your thread is running (figure 2).

5 Continue this until you get to the beginning of your circle. Pass your needle through the first bead added in this round (figure 3).

6 String one bead and pass your needle through the next bead in the previous row. Continue this all around and repeat from * on figure 3.

To Add Pattern

7 After you have a few rows to work from, introduce a new color of bead. For this necklace, we used green. Follow the pattern adding beads in a diagonal in the following order: brown, green, red, yellow, purple, red, and repeat.

To Change Thread

8 When you have about 6 to 10 inches (15.2 to 25.4 cm) left on your working thread, weave it back through your beadwork several times and snip away the remaining thread. To add new thread, cut a new piece of beading thread and thread the needle. Begin by weaving your thread in a zigzag motion and come out of the last bead where your previous working thread began to get buried. You are ready to continue on.

To Add the Clasp

9 Where your thread comes out of the last delica, run your needle through one of the large beads, through the loop of the clasp, back down through the large bead and back through the adjacent delica, then repeat this step. Continue this until you have made a complete circle. Weave your thread back through your beadwork and cut the thread.

10 Repeat step 9 on the other side.

YOU WILL NEED

Nylon beading thread, size D

Beeswax or thread conditioner

Beading needle, size 10**

Size 11 delicas, 6 grams of brown, green, purple, and red, and 9 grams of yellow*

Pencil

Scissors

2 beads with large hole, each 12 mm in diameter

Hook-and-eye jewelry clasp

*A type of cylindrical bead. Use delicas (as opposed to regular seed beads) because they are more uniform in shape and their thin walls and large holes can accommodate multiple threads.

**Use a beading needle because it's thin and flexible, and the eye is so small it can pass through small beads.

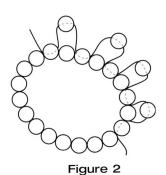

Figure 1

Figure 2

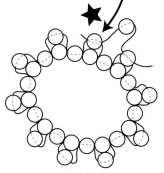

Figure 3

One Pill Makes You Bigger, One Pill Makes You Small

arvard professor Timothy Leary entreated the youth of the '60s to tune in, turn on, and drop out. Bob Dylan proclaimed that "everybody must get stoned." The Beatles waxed psychedelic about "Lucy in the Sky with Diamonds." It seemed like all the icons of the hippie movement were having some far-out experiences with recreational drugs, and they wanted to spread the news and share the sensation with their fans and followers.

Just a decade before, marijuana, then called dope or reefer, had been considered the exclusive province of shady, underworld "dope fiends" and other undesirables, such as communists and jazz musicians. The writers of the Beat Generation (who were also big fans of jazz) came along in the '50s and openly admitted to using the drug, praising its natural, mellowing high and convincing their fans that smoking pot didn't lead to crime sprees, as federal authorities had claimed. Smoking pot soon became a political statement, just another way the young generation chose to challenge authority and do their own thing.

While pot was the drug of choice for those seeking a natural high, LSD (lysergic acid diethylamide) went further, producing a chemically driven experience described as a trip. Acid, as it came to be known, was developed in the '40s as

Karen smoking a pot pipe.
© HENRY DILTZ/CORBIS

Pass it over

a way of helping psychiatrists understand schizophrenia. As psychiatrists learned more about the drug, which produced colorful hallucinations, some became convinced that it could be used for "mind expansion," leading to greater consciousness. Timothy Leary became the drug's leading champion, testing it on famous artists, such as Allen Ginsberg, and taking it himself. The more he took LSD, Leary claimed, the closer he got to God, and he founded the League of Spiritual Discovery, a society dedicated to expanding consciousness through the use of LSD. Soon

SMOKING POT DIDN'T LEAD TO CRIME SPREES

Leary had many followers (millions had reportedly taken LSD by 1964), including the Beat writers Cassady and Jack Kerouac, who developed the first public "acid test" in 1964. Cassady and his Merry Pranksters held a happening and put LSD in the food and beverages so that everyone attending could "turn on;" be free from their inhibitions, and reach new levels of consciousness and creativity. While those taking acid saw fantastic visions and heard inanimate objects speak, those looking on saw what looked like a bunch of crazy people babbling incoherently, sometimes injuring or even killing themselves while tripping. After a few highly publicized deaths due to LSD, the drug became illegal in 1966, a move which may have only contributed to its popularity in the late '60s.

By the end of the decade, harder and more addictive drugs such as heroin had hit the streets, and the increase in drug addiction and drug-related crimes brought to light the very real and damaging effects of illegal drugs.

Allen Ginsberg amongst protesters at a marijuana rally.
© BETTMAN/CORBIS

to me again...

WEAVING & YARN CRAFTS

Not quite as meditative as yoga, but almost, yarn crafts became very popular with hippies and other creative types in the '60s. The materials were inexpensive, and the crafts had the right kind of earthy appeal. Those who couldn't afford a loom could make their own simple cardboard loom and still create impressive designs. Latch-hooking rugs, pillows, and wall hangings also became a popular way to be creative, and everybody knew how to make a simple woven god's eye. The designs in this section update the old hippie favorites with interesting new colors and patterns.

PHOTO COURTESY OF JEAN RAY LAURY AND JOYCE AIKEN

Shawl by Dorothy Smaller.

DESERT DREAM CATCHER

Designer: KATHRYN TEMPLE

Dream catchers, a common tradition in several Native American cultures, were adopted by hippies drawn to their spiritual meaning. According to legend, while humans sleep, dreams float over their heads. The bad ones get caught in the dream catcher's web so that they won't affect the sleeper.

1 Bend the vines into a round wreath. Continue adding vines, overlapping and weaving until the wreath holds its shape on its own. As the vines dry out over time, the shape will hold together easily.

2 Cut a long piece of dental floss and tie one end to the wreath (figure 1).

3 To create the "web," pull the floss about 2 inches (5.2 cm) to the right of the original knot. Wrap it once around the wreath and then feed it back through the semicircle "hole" you just created. Do not pull the floss completely taut. You want it to have a little give. Continue

this process until you've worked your way almost all the way around the wreath (figure 2).

4 For your second pass around the wreath, knot the floss at the midpoint of each length of floss, rather than to the wreath.

5 Continue spiraling inward until you have the reached near the center.

6 Tie a double or triple knot to secure the floss (figure 3).

7 Next, use small pieces of floss to tie beads at various points in the web. Trim the floss.

8 Finally, cut three pieces of floss and double knot them at the bottom of the wreath. Thread them with beads and tie feathers to the ends.

Variation

This simple peace sign wreath is made from bending pliable vines into a circle and tucking the ends under, then positioning a found branch in the center. Finding just the right branch is a fun part of the project.

YOU WILL NEED

Pliable vines, such as grapevine*

Dental floss

Beads

Scissors

Feathers

*Use freshly cut vines, if possible, or buy them in a craft store and soak them in water overnight.

Figure 1

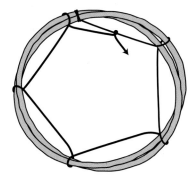

Figure 2

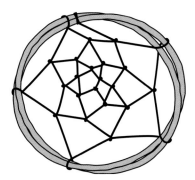

Figure 3

COSTA DEL SOL BELT

Designer: KATHRYN TEMPLE

Over, under, over, under. Once you've got the rhythm of cardboard loom weaving, you'll be able to weave just about anything. This simple sash is a good first project to try.

1 First, create your loom. Use the ruler and pencil to make at least 10 marks (about 1/4 inch [6 mm] apart) on each narrow end of the mat board. Make sure the marks on each side of the board match up, as you'll need them to be accurate for successful weaving.

2 Cut each of the marks about 1/2 inch (1.3 cm) deep with your craft knife to create notches for the loom.

3 Cut 10 pieces of yarn of equal length. Cut the pieces at least 6 inches (15.2 cm) longer than the desired finished length of your belt.

4 Make a double knot 3 inches (7.6 cm) from the end of each of the 10 strands of yarn. Feed the first piece of yarn through the left-hand notch at the top of your loom. The knot should be pulled firmly against the back of the mat board. Pull the yarn taut and feed it through the corresponding notch at the bottom of your mat board. Continue until you have threaded all 10 pieces of yarn to your loom (figure 1).

7 Turn the knife on its edge. Thread your yarn through the hole in the ruler. Use the ruler as a shuttle, threading the yarn in the ruler's hole between the strands of yarn on the loom (figure 2).

8 Return the knife to a flat position and use it to "comb" the yarn down toward the knotted edge of the loom.

9 Slide the knife to the top of your loom.

10 Use your second knife to weave the opposite pattern of the first knife (under, over, under, over).

You Will Need

Plastic ruler with a hole in it

Pencil

Mat board, about 8 x 12 inches (20.3 x 30.5 cm)

Craft knife

Scissors

Thin yarn in three different colors

2 toothless butter knives

Bulldog clip

Large-eye needle

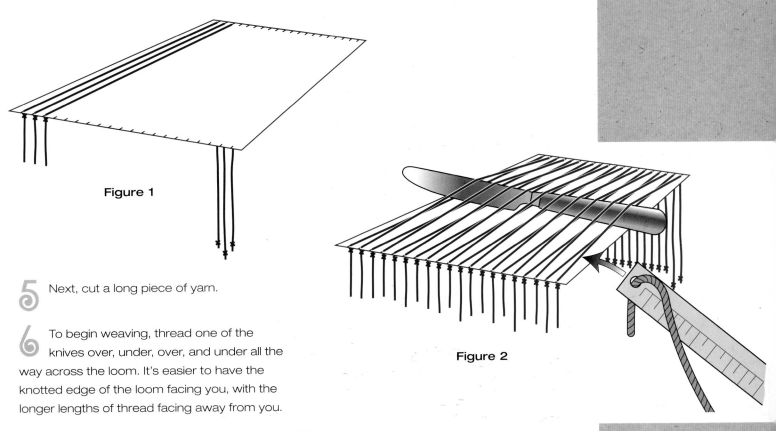

Figure 1

5 Next, cut a long piece of yarn.

6 To begin weaving, thread one of the knives over, under, over, and under all the way across the loom. It's easier to have the knotted edge of the loom facing you, with the longer lengths of thread facing away from you.

Figure 2

11 Repeat the shuttle and combing process.

12 Continue weaving until your piece of yarn runs out or you are ready to change colors. You'll save time by keeping one knife "woven" at all times, moving it to the top of the loom as you reweave the second knife.

13 When you are ready to change colors, weave the last part of your yarn into the middle of the sash; don't let it dangle out the side. Overlap the weaving of the next color by a few strands of yarn.

14 Continue until you run out of room on your loom.

15 Next, carefully tie off the first end of your belt (on the knotted side of your loom). Double knot your end strands of yarn two at a time until you have created a fringe all the way across.

16 Now, slip off the loom yarn on the opposite end. Slide your belt down on the loom. Secure the woven end with a bulldog clip and then refeed each of the 10 strands of yarn through the notches in the other end (figure 3)

17 Continue this process until you have reached the desired length.

18 Tie the end yarn off as before to create fringe.

19 Use a large-eye needle to weave in any dangling yarn on the back of the belt.

YESTERDAY'S WEAVING

Neck piece by Candace Crocket
PHOTO COURTESY OF JEAN RAY LAURY AND
JOYCE AIKEN

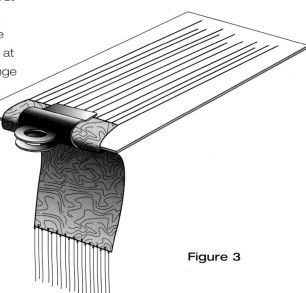

Figure 3

EARTHY PURSE

Designer: KATHRYN TEMPLE

The nubby texture of this purse makes it charming and appealing—perfect with a peasant dress or a poncho. The directions are for a small purse, but you can make a bigger one by creating a larger cardboard loom.

Plastic ruler with a hole in it

Pencil

Mat board, at least 8 x 12 inches (20.3 x 30.5 cm)

Craft knife

Yarn in several different colors*

Scissors

2 toothless butter knives

Large-eye yarn needle

Thick yarn for strap

*Worsted-weight is a good size to use. If this is your first time weaving, use the same size yarn for your warp (base) and your weaving. Once you have the hang of it, use whatever type of yarn you wish for weaving. For this project, the designer used maroon, yellow, and bright blue.

1. First, create your pocket loom. Use the ruler and a pencil to make at least 30 marks, 1/4 inch (6 mm) apart, on each short end of the mat board. Make sure the marks on each side of the board match up, as you'll need them to be accurate for successful weaving.

2. Cut each of these marks about a 1/2 inch (1.3 cm) deep with the craft knife to create notches in the board.

3. Using a yarn of average thickness for your warp, cut 30 pieces of equal length. The yarn should be about 2 to 3 inches (5.1 to 7.6 cm) longer than the length of the board.

4. Make a double knot about 2 inches (5.1 cm) from one end of each length of yarn. Feed one length of yarn through the first notch at the top of your loom. The knot should be pulled firmly against the back of the mat board. Pull the piece of yarn taut across the length of the board and feed it through the corresponding notch on the other end of your loom (figure 1, page 117). Continue until you have threaded all 30 pieces of yarn onto your loom.

5. To begin weaving, thread one of the knives over, under, over, and under, all the way across the loom at the unknotted edge. It's easier to do this with the knotted edge of the loom facing you.

6. Cut a 36-inch (91.4 cm) piece of yarn to weave with. Thread one end of the yarn through the hole in the plastic ruler.

7. Turn the knife on its edge and, using the ruler as a shuttle, thread your first color of yarn between the warp (figure 2, page 117).

8. Return the knife to a flat position and use it to "comb" the yarn down toward the knotted edge of the loom. Slide the knife back to the top of your loom.

9. Use the second knife to weave the opposite pattern of the first knife (under, over, under, over). Turn the knife on its edge.

10. Thread the ruler shuttle through the warp and comb the yarn against the previous row.

11. Remove the knife you just turned on its edge. You will save time by keeping one knife "woven" at all times, moving it to the top of the loom as you reweave with the second knife.

12. Weave four or five rows of your "base" color. Continue weaving until your piece of yarn runs out or you are ready to change colors.

13. To begin the square in the center of the purse, weave your base color seven threads in. Run your base color under the middle 16 rows on your loom. Then weave the last threads on the opposite side. Repeat this process back and forth for about 16 rows.

14. You'll find it easier to weave the yellow square using your large needle to hold the yarn. Weave four rows of the yellow yarn in the unwoven 16 strands.

15. For the fifth through twelfth rows, weave the yellow yarn through the first five yarns of the middle section, weave it under the middle six yarns, then continue weaving through the last five yarns of the middle section. Repeat this process for seven additional rows (eight total). For the next four rows, weave the yellow yarn through all 16 yarns.

16. Finally, to weave the cobalt blue square, thread the needle with your yarn and weave back and forth on the remaining six middle yarns for eight rows.

17. Continue weaving with your base color until you have woven a rectangle. The rectangle will be folded in half, so the middle of your weaving marks the bottom crease of the purse. Adjust the size of your rectangle as desired.

18. Knot your end strings together two at a time until you have created a fringe all

the way across both edges. Remove the weaving from the loom.

19 Trim the fringe close to the knots. Thread the yarn needle with yarn in the base color of your purse. Stitch the fringe to the back of your woven piece.

20 Fold the woven rectangle in half, right sides together. Thread the needle with yarn and stitch the short sides together.

21 Next, knot a piece of yarn repeatedly to create a round knot about the size of a small marble for the latch. Use the needle and yarn to sew this to the purse. Sew a loop of yarn to the other side of the purse's opening. This will slip over the knot to fasten the purse closed.

22 Braid three pieces of the thick yarn for the strap of the purse. Use the needle and yarn to sew the strap to the purse.

YESTERDAY'S WEAVING

PHOTOS COURTESY OF JEAN RAY LAURY AND JOYCE AIKEN

Designer: KATHRYN TEMPLE

HOMESPUN SCARF

This scarf has that simple, handmade quality that can only be achieved by weaving. But before you go out and invest in a loom, try your hand at cardboard loom weaving. It's so simple that children often learn it in art class or at camp.

1 First, create your pocket loom. Use the ruler and make at least 20 marks ¼ inch (6 mm) apart on each narrow end of the mat board. Make sure the marks on each side of the board match up, as you'll need them to be accurate for successful weaving. This will create a scarf approximately 5 inches (12.7 cm) wide. Make additional marks to increase the width.

2 With the craft knife, cut each of these marks about a ½ inch (1.3 cm) deep to create notches in the board.

3 Using a yarn of average thickness for your warp, cut 20 or more pieces of equal length. The yarn should be about 8 inches (20.3 cm) longer than the desired length of your scarf. A good scarf length is 30 inches (76.2 cm).

4 Make a double knot 4 inches (10.2 cm) from one end of each length of yarn. Feed one length of yarn through the first notch at the top of your loom. The knot should be pulled firmly against the back of the mat board. Pull the piece of yarn taut across the length of the board and feed it through the corresponding notch on the other end of your loom (figure 1, page 117). Continue until you have threaded all lengths of yarn onto your loom.

5 Cut a 36-inch (91.4 cm) or longer piece of yarn to weave with. Thread one end of the yarn through the hole in the plastic ruler.

6 To begin weaving, thread one of the knives over, under, over, and under, all the way across the loom at the unknotted edge. It's easier to do this with the knotted edge of the loom facing you.

7 Turn the knife on its edge and, using the ruler as a shuttle, thread your first color of yarn between the warp (figure 2, page 117).

8 Return the knife to a flat position and use it to "comb" the yarn down toward the knotted edge of the loom. Slide the knife back to the top of your loom.

9 Use the second knife to weave the opposite pattern of the first knife (under, over, under, over). Turn the knife on its edge.

10 Thread the shuttle through the warp and comb the yarn against the previous row.

11 Remove the knife you just turned on its edge. You will save time by keeping one knife "woven" at all times, moving it to the top of the loom as you reweave with the second knife.

12 Weave four or five rows. Continue weaving until your piece of yarn runs out or you are ready to change colors.

13 When you are ready to change colors, weave the last part of your yarn toward the center of the scarf. Start your next color by overlapping the previous color by a few strings.

14 Continue to weave until you run out of room on your loom.

15 Next, carefully lift your weaving off the loom only at the knotted end.

16 Now, slip the loom strings on the opposite end off. Slide your scarf down on your loom with about 1 inch (2.5 cm) of woven material still on the loom surface. Secure the woven end with a bulldog clip and then refeed each of the 20 strings through the notches in the other end (figure 3, page 118).

17 Continue weaving until you run out of room. Repeat steps 15 and 16, as needed.

18 When you have woven the desired length, tie off end pairs of strings with a double knot to create fringe.

19 Use a large-eye needle to weave in any dangling strings on the back of the scarf.

You Will Need

Plastic ruler with a hole in it

Pencil

Mat board, at least 8 x 12 inches (20.3 x 30.5 cm)

Craft knife

Yarn in several different colors*

Scissors

2 toothless butter knives

Bulldog clip

Large-eye yarn needle

*Knitting worsted is a good size to use. If this is your first time weaving, use the same size yarn for your warp and your weaving. Once you have the hang of it, use whatever type of yarn you wish for weaving. For this project, the designer used maroon, bright blue, and orange.

GOD'S EYE REVISITED

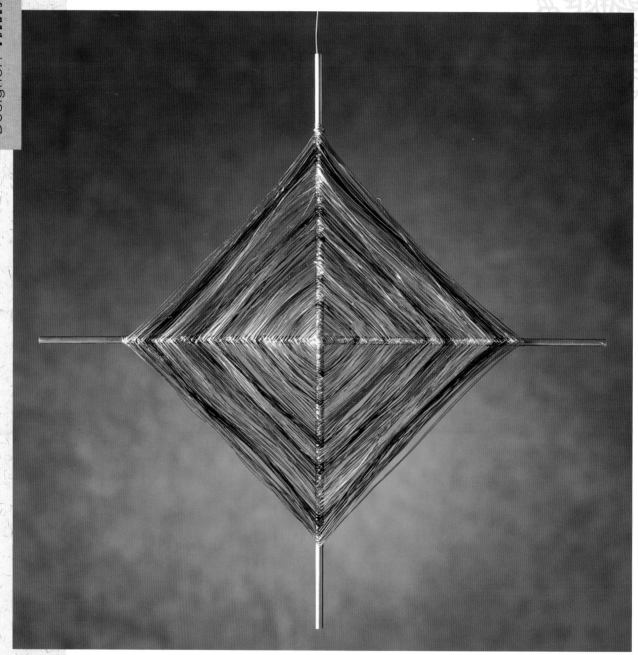

The god's eye or *ojo de dio* was an ancient symbol used by Central American people to protect their homes and keep away evil spirits. In the '60s, god's eyes caught on with the hippie crowd, woven from brightly colored yarn wrapped around simple sticks. This updated version uses copper wire on copper dowels for a sleek modern effect.

1. Use the round file to cut corresponding grooves in the center of each dowel so that they connect. You can solder the dowels together for an extra firm connection if you like (figure 1).

2. Begin wrapping your first color of wire around the dowels according to figure 2.

3. To start a new color of wire, tie the new piece to the end of the previous piece with a double knot and continue the weaving process (figure 3).

4. Continue wrapping the wire around the dowels until you reach about 2 inches (5.2 cm) from the edges of the dowel. Cut the end of the wire and tuck it around the back of the dowel.

YOU WILL NEED

Two 12-inch long (30.4 cm) copper dowels, each about ⅛-inch (3 mm) in diameter*

Round file

Solder gun and solder (optional)

Copper wire, about 12 yards (10 m) of each color

Pliers

*Available at craft stores

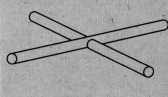

Figure 1

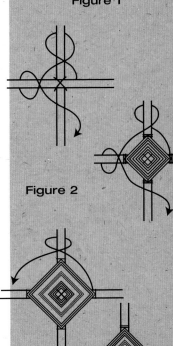

Figure 2

Figure 3

YESTERDAY'S EYE OF GOD

Yarn Sculpture at Human Be-In
PHOTO COURTESY OF STEPHEN SHAPIRO

MELLOW YELLOW LATCH-HOOK PILLOW

Designer: REBECCA C. DEIBER

Who needs furniture when you can sit on the floor on a comfortable latch-hook pillow? When latch hooking was popular in the '60s, crafters created rugs, pillows, wall hangings, and even bedspreads in psychedelic colors and groovy patterns. This design is a little more contemporary, but just as cozy and comfortable.

1 Cut the latch hook canvas into a 25-inch (63.5 cm) square.

2 Using the template as a guide, use the permanent marker to draw the outlines of the design on the latch-hook canvas. To do this, first find the center of both the pattern and your canvas. Now count squares going up, and draw the outlines of the design on your canvas, remembering that each square in the pattern represents one square (actually a hole) in the canvas. Continue to count squares and draw the outlines of the pattern. Leave at least a 1-inch (2.5 cm) border on all sides of the canvas.

3 Now you're ready to begin latch hooking. Remember, each square in the pattern represents one knotted piece of yarn in your finished design. The yarn is actually knotted to the horizontal thread directly above the hole in the canvas (the top line of the square in the pattern). It's important to start latch hooking in the lower left corner of the canvas and then work your way across row by row, not by filling in areas of color. To begin latch hooking, place one strand of yarn around the latch hook, below the latch (figure 1).

4 Remembering to leave a 1-inch (2.5 cm) border, push the hook down through the first hole in the pattern, under the horizontal thread, and up through the hole directly above until the latch is through the hole (figure 2).

5 Pull both ends of the yarn across the shank of the tool, between the hook and the latch, as shown in figure 3.

6 Pull the hook slowly back through the hole. This will cause the latch to close and grab the ends of the yarn, pulling them through the yarn's loop to form a knot.

7 Tighten the knot by tugging gently on the two ends of the yarn (figure 4). You've now completed one knot.

8 Continue latch hooking your way from left to right, row by row up the canvas, until the entire design is filled in.

9 When you've finished hooking the canvas, use the paintbrush to coat the back of the canvas with the rug-backing compound to secure the yarn to the canvas.

10 When the backing compound is dry, iron the rug binding on to the back of the canvas as close to the yarn as possible.

11 Lay the backing fabric right side up on a flat surface. Place the finished hooked canvas yarn side down on the backing fabric. Pin the pieces together and then sew on three sides.

12 Turn the pillowcase inside out. Insert the foam pillow form and sew the fourth side closed.

Figure 1

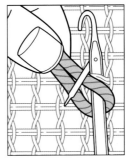

Figure 2

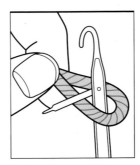

Figure 3

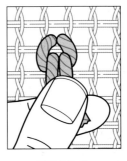

Figure 4

You Will Need

Ruler or measuring tape

Scissors

Latch-hook canvas (enough for 25-inch [63.5 cm] square)

Template on page 143

Permanent marker

Latch-hook rug yarn (about 6 packages avocado, 12 packages honey gold, 5 packages natural)

Latch hook

Paintbrush

Rug-backing compound

Iron

Iron-on rug binding

Fabric for back of pillow (enough for 25 x 25 inch [63.5 cm] square)

Straight pins

20-inch (50.8) square pillow form

While some hippies went trekking off to Asia to find inner peace and a simple life, others pursued the same ideals closer to home, rediscovering rural America as part of the "back to the land" movement. Reversing the twentieth century trend of leaving small towns and farms for cities and factories, thousands of modern-day Thoreaus sought a life of quiet self-sufficiency closer to nature, away from what they saw as an artificial consumer culture.

The beginning of the movement can be credited to the publication of Helen and Scott Nearing's book, *Living the Good Life* (Shocken), in 1954. The book chronicled the Nearing's move to an old farm shack in rural Vermont, where they made or grew everything they needed,

PHOTO COURTESY OF MOTHER EARTH NEWS, 1971
www.motherearthnews.com

eating wild blueberries from the native bushes and constructing fences and a home from fieldstone.

For many hippie types, the Nearing's philosophy was seen as a panacea for the mass consumption that characterized post–World War II America, with its emphasis on convenience and disregard for nature. Being self-reliant was a way to *really* reject the establishment and mainstream values. Hippies sought out cheap property in isolated areas, leaving behind conventions like plumbing, heat, and sometimes even electricity in favor of farmable land or solitude. Publications such as *Mother Earth News* and *The Whole Earth Catalog* spread the gospel of self-sufficiency with articles covering everything from raising geese for money and making your own cleaning products to building a wind-powered washing machine. Back-to-the-landers built their own homes, made their own furniture, grew their own food organically, and went "off the grid," using solar or wind energy instead of electricity. To make enough money to get by, they started cottage industries, such as making candles, soap, or crocheted goods, and sold the products at farmers' markets and co-ops.

Eventually, enough like-minded individuals moved to the same areas, changing the character of the communities, often to the chagrin of the locals. These hippie-friendly areas gained a reputation as hubs of tolerance and hippie ideals, attracting a steady stream of resettlers.

For some who tried the rural way of life, it was a dramatic change. The isolation or difficulty making a living became insurmountable problems,

John Bauer, a wood carver, with Naomi Sun and Maya Moon.
PHOTO COURTESY OF ALEXANDRA JACOPETTI HART AND THE ESTATE OF JERRY WAINWRIGHT

BEING SELF-RELIANT WAS A WAY TO REALLY REJECT THE ESTABLISHMENT

and they returned to more populous areas. By the end of the 1970s, many of the more stringent followers of the back to the land philosophy had relaxed their standards somewhat or altogether, and they began interacting more with the mainstream. At the same time, the back-to-the-lander's values, which had once been seen as radical, began to gain more widespread acceptance. Organic foods, holistic medicine, and alternative energy sources slowly began to catch on within the mainstream of popular culture. Although the back to the land movement as such faded into the past, it was reborn in a new form with the "voluntary simplicity" movement that grew up in response to the consumer excesses of the '80s and '90s.

CANDLEMAKING

ncense, music, and lots of candles were a key part of any hippie happening. Since candles got a lot of use, some folks found themselves going through them pretty quickly, so they learned how to make their own to save money. Candlemaking turned out to be the perfect cottage industry—it was easy to learn, the materials were cheap, and there was an ever-growing market. But hippie candlemakers didn't make your average tapers and church candles. Just like every other aspect of the counterculture, candles were distinctive and reflected hippie style. Those who weren't into the artificial light shows at love-ins and concerts could create their own natural light shows at home with glowing candles in rainbow colors and sculptural shapes. Here are a few easy-to-make candle designs that keep the hippie flame flickering.

Light My Fire
Ice Candle

Designer: Pamela Brown

A hippie classic, ice candles are so easy to make that they're often a project for kids in summer camps. Each ice candle has a completely unique texture. As it melts, an ice candle is transformed into a fascinating sculpture, the perfect thing to contemplate if you're in a meditative mood.

1 Place the wax in the slow cooker on high heat until it melts. Use the thermometer to determine when the temperature reaches 180°F (82°C), then turn down the heat. When the temperature is between 160°F (71°C) and 180°F (82°C), add the stearic acid and stir until it's completely dissolved. Dip the wick quickly into the melted wax to prime it, then set it aside. Maintain the wax at 160°F (71°C).

2 Shave a small amount of dye block into the wax and stir. Add more dye until you reach the desired color.

3 Pull the primed wick through the mold and make sure it's centered. Seal the bottom with mold seal and secure the wick at the top with a pencil or chopstick.

4 Fill the mold with crushed ice. Quickly pour the 160°F (71°C) melted wax over the ice until the mold is full.

5 Let cool thoroughly. Turn the mold over in the sink, allowing the melted ice to pour out. Gently pull the candle from the mold. Allow it to dry completely before lighting. Cut the excess wick at the bottom of the candle and trim the wick on top to ¼ to ½ inch (6 mm to 1.3 cm).

YOU WILL NEED

Paraffin wax, about 1½ lbs. (680 g)*

Slow cooker

Candy thermometer

Stearic acid, about 3 tablespoons (44 ml) per pound (453.5 g) of wax*

Spoon for stirring

Wick (size appropriate to mold)*

Craft knife

Candle dye block*

Candle mold of choice*

Mold seal*

Pencil or chopstick

Crushed ice

Scissors

*Available at craft stores

YESTERDAY'S CANDLES
Moratorium candle, 1969

Goin' Mobile

For carefree, adventurous hippies, being mobile was important, and that meant having the right set of wheels. But the sedans and family wagons of their parents' generation were too square and didn't suit a hippie lifestyle. And so, on highways and back roads around the world, new and characteristically hippie types of transportation started to appear.

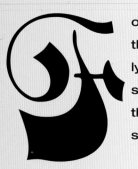

Concertgoers on the roof of Volkswagon bus at the Woodstock Music and Arts fair at Bethel, NY in mid-August, 1969.
© AP/WIDE WORLD PHOTO

The vehicle most strongly associated with hippies was the bus, Volkswagen or otherwise. When Ken Kesey and his Merry Pranksters painted an old school bus with psychedelic murals and dubbed its destination "Further," they started a trend. The group set out across the U.S. moving west to east, and Jack Keruoac chronicled their experiences in *On the Road* (Viking, 1957). Soon other freedom-seekers were adopting the gypsy lifestyle. As Ken Kesey put it, "You're either on the bus, or you're off the bus."

A converted bus, outfitted with floor mattresses and perhaps an electric hot plate, was big enough for up to a dozen people to live in. In fact, over 70 people joined the bus caravan "Out to Save the World," which left San Francisco for The Farm in Tennessee in 1970. Some hippies kept buses in one place as a permanent home; others enjoyed the freedom of being able to pull up roots and find a new place. The Volkswagen camper van (otherwise known as the bus) came with built-in sleeping quarters and a kitchen area, making life a little more comfortable for those who chose it as a home. Whatever the type of bus, it was much cooler if it was hand-painted, the more psychedelic the better. If one had to participate in the mainstream by using a vehicle, at least it could be groovy.

The most popular alternative to a VW bus was a VW Beetle, also known as a "love bug." Marketed as "the people's car," the Beetle was said to have looks only a mother could love. But hippies embraced the quirky German car for its low price and easy maintenance. Beetle engines had the same parts from year to year, so it was easy to find parts and fix your own car—an appealing notion for self-reliant hippies who liked to live outside the system. The occasional intrepid hippie even drove a Beetle or Volkswagen bus from Europe to India, along the great "hippie trail," although it's unclear how many of the cars actually made the journey round-trip.

Finally, for the ultimate in freedom, there was the motorcycle. Who can forget the sight of Dennis Hopper and Peter Fonda roaring through the desert on their choppers in Easy Rider?

No car, no bus, no motorcycle? Why tie yourself down to a vehicle when you can hitchhike? Bumming rides became a common pastime for hippies, perfectly accepted by society until slasher movies in the '70s scared everyone out of it.

As Ken Kesey put it, "You're either on the bus, or you're off the bus."

Hitch-hiking to Minneapolis, 1969

Further, *the Merry Prankster's bus*   © TED STRESHINSHKY/CORBIS

RAINBOW CANDLES

Designer: PAMELA BROWN

You may remember rainbow candles in psychedelic colors and patterns not unlike those found in tie-dyed T-shirts. These candles feature more contemporary colors, but the same great design.

1 Place the wax in the slow cooker on high heat until it melts. Use the thermometer to determine when the temperature reaches 180°F (82°C), then turn the heat to low. When the temperature has dropped to between 160°F (71°C) and 180°F (82°C), add the stearic acid and stir until completely dissolved. Dip the wick quickly into the melted wax to prime it, then set it aside.

2 Fill the pan one-third full of water, place it on the stove, and turn the heat to medium. Separate the wax into batches, according to how many color layers you plan to make. You'll use a different tin can for each color. Pour the wax into the tin cans. Put the tin cans in the pan of water (use a weight, such as a utensil, to hold each can in place).

3 Shave small amounts of dye into each can until you achieve the desired colors.

4 Pull the primed wick through the candle mold and secure it by tying it to a pencil or chopstick. Secure the wick at other end with the mold seal. Place the mold in another container that keeps it stable, or place something under it to stablize it.

5 Pour a small amount of wax into the mold to make the first layer. Allow the wax to cool until there is a film of cooled wax on top. If the layer isn't thick enough, the colors will blend.

6 Repeat step 5 for each layer of color you want to add. When the mold is completely full, let it partially cool. You'll see that an area of suction will create an indent. Fill the indent with the last color, then allow the candle to cool and harden.

7 When the candle is completely cool, untie the wick and pull the candle from the mold. If it won't come out, put it in the refrigerator for an hour and try again. Trim the wick to 1/4 to 1/2 inch (6 mm to 1.3 cm).

Sand Candles

A refreshing change from all the high-tech, expensive candles you see around today, sand candles are easy to make and require only a few simple materials.

1 Fill the bottom of your plastic container with damp sand. The sand should be level, firmly packed, and about 1½ inches (3.8 cm) deep.

2 Put the bowl down on top of the sand and press it gently into place. Make sure that the edges of the bowl are at least 2 inches (5.2 cm) away from the sides of your plastic container.

3 Next, pack damp sand around the bowl until the sand is almost level with the top of the bowl. **Note: The damper the sand, the less it will adhere to the hot wax.

4 Carefully remove the bowl from the sand mold, leaving a bowl-shaped impression in the sand. You'll be filling this area with wax.

5 Melt your wax in a double boiler over medium heat.

6 After the wax has melted, use the carrot peeler to make crayon shavings to tint the wax to the desired color. Stir with the wooden spoon.

7 Cut a piece of wicking at least 2 inches (5.2 cm) longer than the height of the candle.

8 Dip the wick into the wax and hang it for a few moments to allow the wax to stiffen.

9 Using the point of a pencil or chopstick, poke a hole in the center of the bottom of the sand mold.

10 Poke one end of the wicking into the hole and use the end of the pencil to gently pack the sand in around it.

11 Lay a pencil or chopstick across the top of the plastic container and bend the wicking to "hook" over it.

12 When the wax is hot enough (the hotter it is, the thicker the wax "crust" on your candle), gently pour it into the sand mold.

13 As the candle dries over the next hour or two, you may notice that the wax settles and leaves the top surface uneven. To correct this, simply reheat the remaining wax and pour just enough onto the top to even out the surface.

14 Allow the candle to dry overnight.

15 Gently remove the candle from the sand. (Do not lift it by the wick, as it may pull out.)

16 If you like, you can carve out patterns in the sand crust with a knife. A carrot peeler works well for making circles.

You Will Need

Plastic container, at least 6 inches (15.2 cm) deep

Sand

Bowl to shape the sand mold

Wax (beeswax, paraffin, or old used candles)

Double boiler

Carrot peeler (optional)

Crayons for coloring the wax

Wooden spoon

Scissors

Wick appropriate to size of mold*

Pencil or chopstick

*Available at craft stores

Reference

As a refresher course for experienced crocheters and marcamers, the following section provides sketches, diagrams, and instructions for the basic stitches and knots you'll use in the projects in the book.

Crochet Refresher

If you're an experienced crocheter, you probably know the common crochet terms and abbreviations by heart. But if its been a while since you've taken up a hook, here's a guide to refresh your memory. We've also included illustrations of common and some more advanced stitches to help you as you work.

Crochet Abbreviations

beg: begin/beginning

ch: chain

ch sp: chain space

dc: double crochet

ea: each

hdc: half double crochet

hk: hook

inc: increase

lp(s): loop(s)

patt: pattern

rep(s): repeat(s)

sc: single crochet

sk #: skip one or more stitches unless stated otherwise

sl st(s): slip stitch(es)

st(s): stitch(es)

tog: together

yo: yarn over

Crochet Terms

Chain space. To create a space by making a chain between stitches. To stitch in a chain space, pass the hook through the loop of the chain space and complete the stitch.

Brackets [ ]. Work the instructions within the brackets the number of times indicated after the brackets.

Foundation. The beginning chain, into which the first row is crocheted. Begin the first row by crocheting under the two top threads of the chain unless you're working around both sides of the foundation chain. Unless the instructions specify, you can crochet under both threads or just one half of the foundation stitch for the first row.

Parentheses (). Parentheses are used in the same way as brackets. Parentheses enclose instructions which contain a section repeated in brackets. This helps to distinguish one set of repeats from another. Parentheses are also used to indicate variations in the instructions based on different sizes.

Post. The vertical part of the stitch, more evident in double and triple crochet stitches.

Round. A horizontal line of stitches in which the work spirals and there is no step up to the next level. This is found only on round spiraling crochetwork.

Row. A horizontal line of stitches in which a level is completed and there is a step up to the next level. This can be a flat piece worked back and forth or a round piece in which each round is completed before a step up to the next row.

Shell. A group of stitches formed in the same stitch or space.

Step-up or turning chain. The chain or chains used at the beginning of a new row to raise the level of work to the height of the new row you are about to begin. For most projects in this book, the turning chain is not counted as a stitch. Look at the "Patt Notes" at the beginning of each pattern to determine if the turning chain is counted.

On the first row (and all rows) the turning chain is listed at the beginning of the row, rather than as part of the foundation stitches or at the end of the row. It really is a part of the current row, and not the row before.

Weave in end. To pass through the last loop of yarn with a tapestry needle then stitch the tail into the crochetwork for about 2 inches (5 cm), so it's hidden. Stitch back and forth, locking the yarn in place so it won't loosen. Clip the tail close to the crochet work.

Work even. Continue each row in pattern, with no increases or decreases.

Yarn over. To wrap the yarn around the hook from back to front. The abbreviation for this action is yo.

US and European Equivalents

Crochet terminology is different in the US than in European countries. All of the instructions in this book are written using US standards. The following table shows the equivalent European terms.

US Terms	European Equivalents
slip stitch (sl st)	single crochet
single crochet (sc)	double crochet
half double crochet (hdc)	half treble crochet
double crochet (dc)	treble crochet
triple crochet (tr)	double treble

Crochet Hook Sizes

Use the following table as a guide for the hook sizes used in this book. Keep in mind that sizes may vary slightly from company to company and between letter name and metric size. Make your project with whichever size hook gives you the intended gauge.

U.S.	Metric	U.K.
D/3	3.25	10
E/4	3.5	9
F/5	3.75	8
G/6	4	7
H/8	5	6
I /9	5.5	5
J/10	6	4

Stitches

Making a Slip Knot

A slip knot is the first step in almost all crochet projects.

1. Hold the tail of the yarn in your right hand and loop the yarn over itself with the skein-end in your left hand.

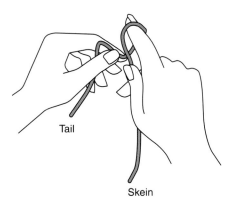

2. With your left hand, push a second loop up through the bottom of the first loop.

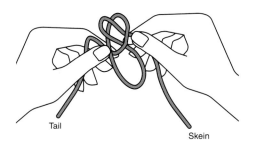

3. Put your hook through the new loop. Tighten the knot by pulling on both ends of the yarn, then pull on the skein end of the yarn to make the slip knot tighten up to the hook.

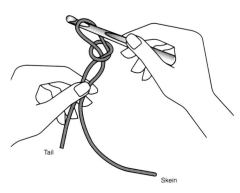

Making a Chain (ch)

Almost every project in this book begins by making a chain of stitches as a foundation for your crochetwork. To make a chain, first make a slip knot. With the hook through the slip knot, wrap the yarn around the hook (yo), and pull it through the slip knot (loop). Repeat this step to make the number of chains indicated in the instructions.

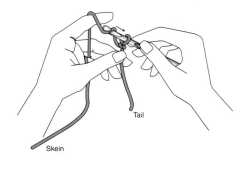

Slip Stitch (sl st)

Push the hook through the second chain from the hook (1 chain and 1 loop on hook).

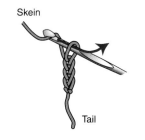

Wrap the yarn around the hook (yo), and pull through both stitches on the hook (1 loop on hook).

Single Crochet (sc)

1. Push the hook through the second chain from the hook (1 chain and 1 loop on hook).

2. Wrap the yarn around the hook (yo), and pull through the chain (2 loops on hook).

3. Wrap the yarn around the hook again, and pull through both loops on the hook (1 loop on hook).

Double Crochet (dc)

1. Wrap the yarn around the hook, insert the hook through the fourth chain from the hook (1 ch and 2 loops on hook).

2. Wrap the yarn around the hook (yo), and pull through the chain (3 loops on hook).

3. Wrap the yarn around the hook (yo), and pull through 2 loops on the hook (2 loops on hook).

4. Wrap the yarn around the hook (yo), and pull through the last 2 loops on the hook (1 loop on hook).

Crocheting into Rows of Stitches

The preceding instructions show you how to begin a row of crochetwork from the foundation chain. To crochet into the following rows of stitches, push the hook through both sides of the top loop on the edge of the fabric, then complete the stitch as usual.

Chain Space (ch sp)

In patterns such as the seed stitch, you'll make a single crochet (sc), then make one chain (ch 1), then make another single crochet two stitches away ("sc in 2nd st," or "skip next st, sc in next st"). The chain between the two single crochet stitches is called a chain space (ch sp). Sometimes, on a following row, you crochet into this chain space (ch sp). This chain space can be any number of stitches between any kind of stitches.

Specialty Stiches

Clusters

For these stitches, you do all but the last yo and pull through of each stitch until the very end. Using clusters, all your stitches end with one yo and pull through, decreasing the group of stitches to one.

2-sc cluster

Insert hk in next st, yo, pull through st, insert hk in next st, yo pull through st, yo, pull through all lps on hk (see figures 1, 2, 3).

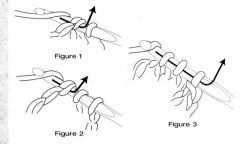

Figure 1

Figure 2

Figure 3

3-dc cluster

[Yo, insert hk in next st, yo, pull through st] 3 times, yo, pull through all lps on hk (see figure 4).

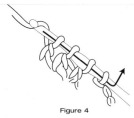

Figure 4

4-dc cluster

[Yo, insert hk in next st, yo, pull through st] 4 times, yo, pull through all lps on hk (see figure 5).

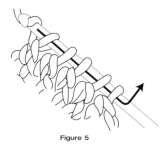

Figure 5

Macrame Refresher

The easiest way to achieve success at macrame is by using the right materials and tools. Luckily, you'll only need a few inexpensive items to get started.

Cord. Depending on your project, you'll want either a thin, flexible cord (best for items like jewelry), or a heavy, sturdy cord (best for items that need to maintain their shape. You can choose from natural fibers (cotton, jute, hemp, sisal, or silk) or synthetic blends (nylon, rayon, etc.).

Knotting board. A piece of foam core is an ideal material for a knotting board. It's inexpensive and can be found at craft, art supply, or office supply stores. The foam core holds T-pins in places, which in turn hold your cord in place. When you're ready to start knotting, cut the board to an easy-to-use size that will fit on your worktable or other workspace (you can even put the board in your lap).

T-pins. These pins (named after their shape) can be found at fabric stores. Just pop them into your foam core and they'll anchor your cords as you work.

Basic Knots

1. Overhand Knot

This is the most basic tying-your-shoes knot. Make a loop. Bring the end of the cord behind the loop and out through the loop. Pull it tight.

2. Coil Knot

This knot is similar to an overhand knot. Make a large overhand knot. Before you close the knot, take one cord and wrap it four times or more around the looped strand, then pull the knot firmly into place.

3. Square Knot

Pass the right-hand cord over the core cords and under the left-hand cords, leaving a little loop on the right. Then pass the left-hand cord under the core cords and up through the loop. Pull the cords to tighten the first half of the knot. Pass the left-hand cord over the core cords and under the right-hand cord, leaving a little loop on the left. Then pass the right-hand cord under the core cords and up through the loop. Pull the cores to tighten the finished knot.

4. Half-Hitch or Half-Knot

This knot is half of the square knot. Instead of passing both left and right-hand cords over the core cords, just do one or the other. This will result in a spiraling cord.

5. Half-Knot Sennit

A continuous chain of half knots will produce a twisting effect. After about four knots, the sennit will begin to twist in the opposite direction from which the knot was started. A full twist requires about eight knots.

6. Diagonal Double Half-Hitch

This is used on a cord that is pulled to a diagonal, rather than remaining vertical. Tie a half hitch around the knot-bearing cord. Tie another half hitch with the same knotting strand around the cord. Pick up the net free knotting strand and repeat.

7. Horizontal Double Half-Hitch

The same process as diagonal, only the knot-bearing cord is held horizontally.

8. Lark's Head Knot

Find the midpoint of your cord and fold it in half, forming a loop. Bring the looped end of the cord under the anchoring cord, ring, buckle, or dowel, from the top. The free ends are placed through the loop and the loop is pulled tight.

9. Josephine Knot

Make a loop in a counterclockwise direction with the left-hand cord so the loop faces to the right. Bring the right-hand cord over the loop and weave it under the lower end of the loop, over the upper end, under the top of the loop, over itself, and finally under the bottom of the loop.

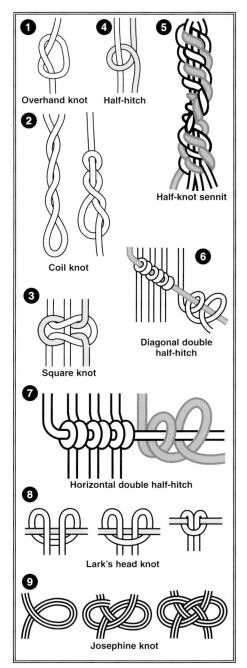

Overhand knot   Half-hitch

Half-knot sennit

Coil knot

Square knot

Diagonal double half-hitch

Horizontal double half-hitch

Lark's head knot

Josephine knot

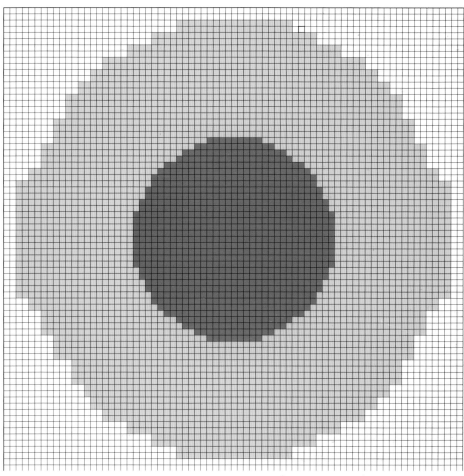

Latch-Hook Pillow, page 126
enlarge 200%

Jeans Patch, page 29

Patchwork Purse, page 28

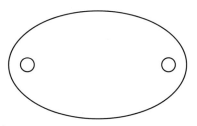

Leather Hair Thong, page 96

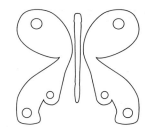

Jeans Patch, page 29
Give Peace A Chance Medallion, page 106

Contributing Designers

Pamela Brown owns a candle store in Asheville, NC where customers oftencomment on the shop being a throwback to the '60s. She says she loved making ice candles as a kid and thought having straight hair and wearing "granny glasses" was the ultimate fashion statement.

Stacey Budge was born the year before the Summer of Love so she's really too young to remember the '60s. But she fondly remembers her favorite pair of orange and brown daisy-covered bell-bottoms, classic Volkswagon beetles, and every lyric from her favorite Janis Joplin album. When she's not designing for Lark Books as an Art Director, this neo-hippie chick can be found crafting and gardening in her home in Asheville, North Carolina.

Lynne Caldwell is a fiber artist living in Asheville, North Carolina. She didn't have much experience with hippie style as a child, but in 1969 (when she was 4) her parents gave in and bought her the most awesome pair of white stretchy go-go boots. Her interest in shibori came much later!

Jane Davis writes books about the crafts she loves, many of which shelearned in the hippie world of the '60s when the "hot" colors were fluorescent lime green, pink. and orange. One of her favorite memories from the '60s was when her dad let her and her sister paint peace signs and flowers on his old red Ford convertible in those "way out" colors.

Rebecca C. Deiber is a proud native of Omaha, Nebraska. During the '60s, she was just a glimmer in her mother's eye, but she does have a pair of Mom's bell-bottoms jeans and loves anything vintage or retro.

Mary Patricia Deprez (Tye Dye Mary®) is celebrating 24 years living and dyeing in Tennessee. Known internationally for her expertise and precision, she began to study the bound resist art medium on The Farm in Summertown, Tennessee. Tye Dye Mary's wearable art is available at he store in Nashville, and through her web site, www.tyedyemary.com.

Jim Gentry has been macraming since the '60s. He teaches workshops and classes in macramé and is the author of The Weekend Crafter: Macramé (Lark Books, 2002).

Georgie Ann Jaggers lives in Asheville, Carolina where she manages a bead store and teaches a variety of beading classes. While she doesn't claim much in the way of hippie credentials, she likes the hippie attitude towards politics, the environment, and creativity.

Joan Morris was in high school in the late '60s, and spent much of her time making crafts just like the ones she made for this book. She is currently the owner of a coffee house in Asheville, NC.

Allison Smith is a frequent contributor to Lark Books and the author of The Girls' World Book of Bath and Beauty (2004). She has a hippie's creative spirit and once lived in a cabin off the grid.

Therese de la Baton Rouge spent the '60s perfecting her ability to draw "bubble letters" on posters and banners exhorting her high school athletic department. In addition, she wrote adolescent poetry while weeping to Jacques Brel and Laura Nyro during her high school years. The early '70s were whiled away with macramé, smoking, and sporadically attending her college classes. She's moved into the twenty-first century as a crafter for Lark Books.

Kathryn Temple is a visual artist and teacher who lives in Asheville, North Carolina. She learned a lot about crafts from her hippie parents.

Acknowledgments

Thanks so much to all our talented designers for coming up with gorgeous contemporary designs that celebrate the best of the hippie era, and doing it on such short notice. Our beautiful models August Hoerr, Loubna Dardane, Deborah Haft, Jesse Mauney, and Abby and Roxanne Semon really helped the designs look their best. Thank you to Katia (Sky) Simonov (skykatia@mac.com), Lisa Mandel and Clarke Snell and Rob Pulleyn for lending us their lovely homes for the photo shoots, and to Mountain Scooters for use of a really cool scooter. Special thanks to Alexandrea Jacopetti Hart and the estate of Jerry Wainwright for the use of their images from Native Funk and Flash (Scrimshaw Press, 1974) and Jean Ray Laury and Joyce Aiken for their wonderful photographs from Creative Body Coverings (Van Nostrand, 1973). Thanks to Helen Heneval for all the wonderful clothes she loaned us for the shoot, and to John Widman for his assistance with props. And most of all to art director Dana Irwin and photographer Sandra Stambaugh for their creativity, dedication, and professionalism under any circumstance.

Index